*This beautifully presented book offers haiku word-picture portraits that provide a tantalizing glimpse into thirty-four therapeutic artist-poets. They share their creative process. Whether art therapist or not—the preponderance of them are—they model the interplay of intrapersonal and interpersonal process. Some of the art alludes to personal loss. Some is sensate and playful. Their creative energies have found an awesome range of outlets—teacher, therapist, professional artist, community activist, founder of programs. Truly for these creators art is life and life is art. Their reflections on the interplay for them of visual and verbal art is captivating and, not surprisingly, diverse. The reader will be fascinated by their lives and inspired by their examples.*

Kenneth P. Gorelick, M.D. RPT
Psychiatrist and clinical poetry therapist
Former Director of Continuing Medical Education
    at St. Elizabeths Hospital
Clinical Professor of Psychiatry at George Washington University

*Editors Cox and Heller stretch a canvas onto which they paint an elegant poem of a form: biographies and essays of seasoned artists/art therapists that speak to and demonstrate the interplay of visual and poetic art. Themes of sacredness, pain, beauty, memory, and connection weave through the stories and are echoed in the creative works. A rare invitation into the soul of creativity, this book soars with numinous grace. I emerged changed.*

Kathleen Adams, MA, LPC, RPT-M/S
Registered poetry/journal therapist
Director, Center for Journal Therapy, Denver

"The faculty of creating is never given to us all by itself. It always goes hand in hand with the gift of observation. And the true creator may be recognized by his ability to find about him, in the commonest and humblest things, items worthy of note."

—Igor Stravinsky (1882-1971)

"We inhabit a deeply imagined world that exists alongside the real physical one. Even the crudest utterance, or the simplest, contains the fundamental poetry by which we live. This mind fabric, woven of images and illusions, shields us.

—Diane Ackerman
from *Deep Play*

# Portrait of
# the Artist
## as Poet

**Edited by Carol Thayer Cox and Peggy Osna Heller**

Magnolia Street Publishers
Chicago, Illinois

*Published by*
Magnolia Street Publishers
1250 West Victoria Street
Chicago, Illinois 60660

ISBN: 1-890374-05-9
Library of Congress Catalog Card No.: pending

Cover Art: Mari Fleming
Book Design: June Padgett, Bright Eye Designs

Printed in the United States of America
2 3 4 5 6 7 8 9 10

COVER
*Of Time, Nature & the Space Between* by Mari Fleming
Beeswax, oil pigment, ginkgo leaves on board, 48" x 66" x 3"

# Creativity Expressed Through Portrait and Poetry

We have entered a period when art has been informing science in new ways, especially through the impact of creative expression on the course of health and illness. Creativity itself has been gaining further understanding. Through my research, I view creativity as built into the species. We witness it in the young child who turns a bed into a sailing ship, and pillows into fortresses. We see it as well in the pursuits of adults of all ages who want to figuratively or literally climb mountains and reach for the stars. We see it in centenarians confronting the upper limits of our life span with their own kind of courage.

The definition I use for creativity is a variation of that used by Rollo May in his book *The Courage To Create*—bringing something new into existence that is valued. Page after page in *Portrait of the Artist as Poet* brings something new into existence of value, visually and verbally.

Through the wonderful legacy of cave paintings, we have known since ancient man and woman that art touches the soul and liberates the human spirit, telling our personal stories and contributing to our sense of well being. Moving from the ancient cave to the modern lab, today's scientists have been identifying how the creative experience results in positive health responses, via the influence of our mind on our brain, as identified in the growing field of psychoneuroimmunology (PNI). Modern science has also been pointing to the positive role of the creative experience in influencing our genes. Many view genes, the key structural elements of our nature, as being separate from factors that contribute to our nurture. But the latest findings from neuroscience show that the challenging influence of human experience typically activates latent genes, like a switch turning on a light. Neuroscientists have discovered that stimulating experiences induce the sprouting of new dendrites, the branchlike extensions of neurons that improve communication within the brain and connections leading to new ideas. Creative endeavors are, of course, among the most powerful of human experiences. They contribute strongly to the creative dance between nature and nurture, to the catalytic interaction between the beauty of the human experience and the biology of the human genome.

This same science and my own research show that there is no upper age limit to creative expression. *Portrait of the Artist as Poet* does the same. The artists in this book range in age from their 30s to their 80s, with their mean age around sixty. The multi-site national "Creativity and Aging" study I am conducting, under the lead sponsorship of the National Endowment for the Arts, is showing active participatory involvement in the arts as having strong health promoting effects on a group of older adults with an average age of 80. The oldest is a 103-year-old poet.

Creativity is perhaps the most defining aspect of the human condition, and arguably its most revitalizing. *Portrait of the Artist as Poet* poignantly and passionately brings these points home. Carol Cox and Peggy Heller have done a laudatory job in bringing this wonderful book to fruition.

Gene D. Cohen, M.D., Ph.D.
Director of the Center on Aging, Health & Humanities
at George Washington University
Author of *The Creative Age* and of *The Mature Mind*

"As imagination bodies forth
The forms of things unknown, the poet's pen
Turns them to shapes, and gives to airy nothing
A local habitation and a name."

—Wm. Shakespeare
*from A Midsummer Night's Dream*


"What was any art but a mold in which to imprison
for a moment the shining elusive element which is life
itself—life hurrying past us and running away, too sweet
to lose."

—Willa Cather (1876-1947)
from *The Song of the Lark*

The editors, Carol Thayer Cox, art therapist, and Peggy Osna Heller, poetry therapist, are published in their respective fields and have served on the editorial boards of professional journals. Cox is the former assistant director of the Art Therapy Program of George Washington University; Heller is former president of the National Association for Poetry Therapy (NAPT) and the NAPT Foundation, president of the National Federation for Biblio/Poetry Therapy, and directs the Wordsworth Center for Growth and Healing.

## ACKNOWLEDGMENTS

The publication of our book has been partially financed through charitable contributions to the National Association for Poetry Therapy Foundation, a non-profit corporation. We, in turn, will donate all of our profit from the sales of this first edition of our book to the Foundation to further its work in support of creative arts therapy. We wish to acknowledge our generous colleagues, friends, and families for believing in this venture and contributing to our bringing it to life.

The Founders' Fund for Art Therapy Education
Virginia Coalition of Arts Therapies Association
Annette Cline
C. James Coakley
Ellen Roth Deutsch
Mimi Farrelly-Hansen
Paula Felder
Donnelle Goplen
Bonnie Hartenstein
Gary and Faye Hussion
Frances Kaplan
Judith S. Lavendar
Wendy Maiorana
Beverley McDaniels
Wendy Lynn Miller
Barbara Sobol Robinson
Tana Sommer

Our gratitude goes to June Padgett of Bright Eye Designs, whose enthusiasm for our project equaled our own and whose aesthetic vision exceeded our expectations. We appreciate Kimberly Cox's meticulous and invaluable editorial proofreading of our manuscript.

"To find ourselves spoken for in art gives dignity to our pain, our anger, our lust, our losses. We can hear what we hope for and what we most fear, in the small release of cadenced utterance.

—Marge Piercy
from Introduction to *Circles on the Water*


"It is art that makes life, makes interest, makes importance…and I know of no other substitute whatever for the force and beauty of its process."

—Henry James (1843-1916)
from a letter to H.G. Wells, July 10, 1915

# ARTIST/POETS

Josie Abbenante.....................................................................2

Cara Barker ...........................................................................6

Joan Bloomgarden .................................................................12

Mildred Lachman Chapin........................................................16

Mary Davies Cole ..................................................................21

Carol Thayer Cox...................................................................27

Ellen Roth Deutsch.................................................................33

Joseph C. Di Bella..................................................................38

Audrey Di Maria.....................................................................43

Mimi Farrelly .........................................................................47

Mary-Michola Fibich ..............................................................53

Mari Marks Fleming ...............................................................58

Pierre A. Grégoire...................................................................64

Bonnie Hartenstein.................................................................68

Sirkku M. Sky Hiltunen...........................................................73

Judith Eisenstadt Horwich.......................................................77

Frances F. Kaplan....................................................................81

Carol Hunter Kelley................................................................87

Sue Kuff ................................................................................91

Carole Kunkle-Miller...............................................................96

Joan Critz Limbrick ..............................................................100

Linsay Locke ........................................................................104

Wendy Maiorana ..................................................................108

Theresa Kress Marks..............................................................112

Linda McQuinney ................................................................116

Wendy Miller .......................................................................120

Joseph Munley .....................................................................126

Concetta Panzarino ..............................................................131

Barbara Sobol Robinson .......................................................135

Tana Sommer .......................................................................139

Ruth Stenstrom ....................................................................144

Christine Vertein ..................................................................150

David G. Vickers ..................................................................154

Katherine J. Williams.............................................................160

In memory of our mothers, Miriam Mendelson Freundlich (1912 – 1998) and Sylvia Ott McGrath (1915 – 2005), whose artistic vision and aesthetic spirit welcomed our own. Both shared with us their love of the simple beauty of everyday things. When we tried our hands at artistic composition, no creative mess went without admiration; no sing-song ditty was dismissed. Our formal education in the arts grew out of such encouragement, and engendered our own commitment to the education of others.

Miriam and Peggy

Sylvia and Carol

As expressive therapists, we are curious about artistic process. We wonder what makes a creative person translate ideas and feelings into this or that art form. Why a poem here, and a painting there?

Why free verse rather than rhyme, or abstraction rather than representation? We have questioned what generates the spark leading to artistic composition, and how it differs for each artist.

We wanted to create a visually dynamic and transformative book that would explore these issues. Images and words: these are the raw materials of communication. They are the natural tools for expressing our basic internal and interpersonal dialogue. In this regard, we are all artists and poets, and we hoped there would be enough interested artists and poets to contribute to such a venture.

To find out, we decided to advertise in a professional newsletter for poetry written by visual artists. The results were encouraging; the respondents were enthusiastic, and their submissions covered a broad range of perspective and style. We subjected the materials to blind review and selected those we considered appropriate. Our subsequent editing launched a reciprocally inspiring ten-year dialogue between us and the contributors.

*Portrait of the Artist as Poet* comprises the work of 34 visual artists who write poetry. Full-color representations of the artists' paintings, collages, drawings, or sculpture are juxtaposed with their poetic compositions to provide an intimate glimpse of the aesthetic practitioner at work. Other books have combined the visual and word art of creative people. What makes *Portrait* unique is that it includes an essay by each contributor titled, "Making Art/Making Poetry: The Variables of Process," a prose reflection on his or her creative and therapeutic process.

It has fascinated us to learn how diverse are the variables of process for the artist/ poets we have met as we engaged in this project. We marveled at the novel vision of the contributors evident in the juxtapositions of their art and poetry. Our work as editors has been a labor of love, fueled by our certainty that this book would have significance as affirmation of the value of creativity.

Coming from across the United States and Canada, the artists whose biographies and photographs accompany their work present North American culture from a variety of perspectives. This is an age of poetic revival. Readings and slams are crowded with people eager to learn more about the art and the artist, often as a way of learning more about themselves.

*Portrait of the Artist as Poet* brings to life the extraordinary vision and voice of some of the people who use these ordinary forms to show and tell their lives, bringing into sharper focus our own. We invite readers of *Portrait* to connect with their personal muse.

— Carol and Peggy

# Josie **Abbenante**

Josie Abbenante, a registered, board certified and licensed art therapist, has taught and practiced art therapy for the last twenty-five years. She added sand-play to her work ten years ago. After graduating from Rice University in pre-med and fine arts, Josie worked with emotionally disturbed teens in a year-round camp setting. The work and her own life experience led her to return to school at the University of Louisville for her master's degree in art therapy.

Abbenante directed art therapy programs at the University of New Mexico and Seton Hill College and also taught at Eastern Virginia Medical School. She has been a visiting faculty member at Vermont College, Mount Mary College, Naropa University, and St. Stephen's College, and currently works with the distance program in art therapy at Pratt Institute. She has presented nationally as well as internationally, traveling to Japan and Canada for art therapy work-shops and teaching. Her practice as an art therapist includes work with the New Mexico School for the Deaf, as well as hospitals, agencies, and private practice.

Josie grew up in Texas and New York in a large family and maintains close ties with her immediate family as well as with her birth daughter, Joannah, and Joannah's family. Their meeting over ten years ago was a gift and their relation-ship continues to bring joy. Other pleasures in her life include time with her whippets and with her husband Peter, bowling (where she and Peter met!), art making, personal sandplay, the outdoors, and New Mexico where she currently resides. Transition has been ongoing, and trusting the transitional space has become a necessity as well as a topic of exploration in her personal and profes-sional work.

The art making is first. The image arrives in various forms and the poetry is its voice. The image describes in the language of metaphor. I am not writing about the image, not explaining or justifying it.

Rather, the image speaks for itself metaphorically and I am listening. I attend to formal qualities (line, light, color, form, space, aesthetics), to content, to relationships within, and to the actual making. Staying with the image in this way results in poetry.

Art making is a means of connecting to self. This has been my experience since age four when relationships with peers and parents became difficult. A long distance move away from close friendships, attending school before I was ready, and the birth of eight more siblings intensified feelings of separation. The anxiety of separation removed me from self and art making reconnected me. I could not have explained that then but now know that the internal quieting and the "losing me" in the creative process is about finding myself.

Making art is visceral. To push and pull the media, tear away, pound out, to be up to my elbows in paint or clay, grounds me physically. That physical grounding quiets my mind and an image forms of its own accord. If ego is in the way, trying to control outcome, then further letting go is necessary. So I shift something—change materials, switch to my non-dominant hand,

close my eyes, work with a "mistake," or change art form and allow music or movement to return me to image making.

Reflecting on the image brings me back to self. I have been formed and reformed by art making. Listening metaphorically further defines the relationship with myself, which I sometimes lose touch with in my everyday driven behavior. When I am stopped by art making and listen to image, I can then hear the words, the definition, the bringing into focus what is available to me.

"Held" is a brief poem that evolved from two images in a series of drawings. I had not intended to draw about or focus on the daughter I had released for adoption twenty-one years earlier, but the images that arrived demanded attention to that event. The images defined themselves as I wrote, returning me to that experience. "Still Life" was written to describe an event. As noted by James Hillman, images are all around us; describing them, listening for the metaphor, "turns the event into experience."

This process of making, describing, and reviewing is grounding and reconnects me to self every time.

*Transition* by Josie Abbenante
Colored pencil, 9″ x 9 1/2″

## HELD

Rising into night
With daylight a blossoming
Look for solid ground

Finding my footing
Seed pearl held in the balance
Pregnant opening

## STILL LIFE

She wanted to learn to do still life,
To draw upon the artist in her self.
Flowers, tree outside the window,
path through the mountains
called her.

Struggling with chalk against paper,
she smeared tree into flowers,
into path.... Nothing
was clear.

It was clear
that nothing
was what she wanted.

The flowers, the tree, the path
led her into the stillness
of life,
and her artist self.

# *Cara* **Barker**

Cara Barker is an author, artist, nurse practitioner, and Jungian Analyst. Maintaining a private practice and a working studio for intergenerational clients in Bellevue, Washington, Dr. Barker is an adjunct professor at Seattle University's Psychology Department. There and elsewhere, Cara is devoted to working with people towards their individuation through creative process.

Trained as an analyst at the C. G. Jung Institute in Kusnacht, Switzerland, Barker explored the role of symbolism in those who experience what she has coined, "world weariness." Her published study, *World Weary Woman: Her Wound and Transformation,* examines the profound effect of trauma and loss upon achievement-driven women who found creative activity essential for survival. Since its publication, the work has prompted speaking invitations from China, Japan, Africa, Europe, and across the United States. Following the September 11, 2001 attacks, Barker's discussions of the plight and redemption of world-weary women and men of all ages led to her published essays, "Where Do I Go From Here?" and "Living on the Edge."

Educated in the fields of speech, nursing, clinical psychology, and expressive arts at the University of Washington, University of California, and Union Institute, Cara is appreciative of the interface of mind, body, and spirit.

Dr. Barker is well known as a pioneer in the realm of spiritual development through the doorway of creative mastery. An intermodal artist, she has had work featured in shows nationally and abroad. Cara lives with her husband in Kirkland, Washington.

For me, making art, whether poetic or visual, means entering the domain of the sacred. It is a kind of quest for soul, that most authentic expression of self.

I have observed three distinct forces that activate my creative process. The first is a yearning for—and openness to—something beyond my need to achieve. The second is the desire to transform chaos, to make some sense of it. And the third is a deeply primordial urge to create.

When I am open artistically and have no agenda, no idea where I am going, I can venture into unmapped territory. If I do not consciously decide upon subject matter, I can wait to see what whispers to me. My job then is to listen, follow, and attend. As I detach from expectations, I move into a state of grace that feels natural, and my artistic process flourishes; product is inconsequential.

The pain of chaos—internal, external, or both—can lead the way to art. My need to find meaning out of incomprehensible loss and suffering requires courage. But when I step up to chaos and dare to enter that which I most want to deny, I am aided by a wise, inner knowing that guides my artistic process.

My urge to create always involves danger, a letting go of what is known and familiar. Just as my Finnish grandfather, Mattias, climbed down into the iron mine each day of his working life, I am compelled to delve into my inner life to search for what holds value in my archaeological dig for soul and substance. Each time I enter the sacred domain of art, I risk coming up empty-handed, with nothing to show for my labors. Sometimes it seems there are only caves of fool's gold. At other times, I am humbled by the rich veins I find, and I must confront the limitations of what my skills can bring to the surface.

Regardless of which force moves me to create, I change and am changed in the process. Whatever the medium with which I am making art, whether with words or with paint, I am also aware that art is making me.

*Ever Present* by Cara Barker
Oil, 36" x 48"

# FOR MY DAUGHTER

For my daughter:
      I want no girdle—
    no manmade,
         nor self-made contraptions
            that cut her breath and bind her soul.

For my daughter:
      I want freedom to breathe—
         and wind bearing witness to her Soul,
            her voice,
               her offering to her community.

For my daughter:
      I want my life to make hers a little gentler,
         if I can—
            more loving,
            more affirming than my own.

For my daughter:
      I want my son's death not to have been in vain—
         but as reminder
            to never forget,
               never, ever forget
                  that those we love,
                     and those who've loved
                        us back
                live on,
                  live in,
                    live through
            our journey through this labyrinth.

For my daughter:
      I want her to know that it is not what she does
         nor whom she knows
            that defines her worth or lovability.
      I want her to know that it is the who she is
         that helps me remember
            the what it is that matters most.

# REMEMBER WHEN WE USED TO IRON?

Remember when we used to iron?
When Monday was the day to shop,
          Tuesday was the day to wash, to clean?
'Til along came Wednesday—
          the time to starch,
                    to press,
                              to fold,
                                        to sort,
                                                  to put away in nice tidy drawers,
                                                            until the next go 'round again?

Remember when we used to iron?
When ironing boards and irons,
          and dust rags and mops
                    gave definition,
                              gave job description
                                        to the hours, the minutes
                                                  and to the days
                                                            of our existence,
          while all the time we waited for who knows what
                    to happen who knows when.
Remember when we used to iron?
What were the dreams that whistled through our hearts
          like cargo on the nearby train,
                    clackety clack along the tracks
                              through our simple minds,
                                        our youthful minds,
                                                  our disciplined minds...
                                                  minds
                                                  so hidden from even us
                                                  beneath our pillbox hats
                                        and white cotton gloves
                                                  on Sunday?

          Perhaps a hope for Camelot?
          Perhaps that in the end, if we were patient,
                    some action would come riding in,
                              some reason to exist
                                        beyond the hangers of well-pressed
                                                  sleeves and colors
                                                            of his shirts
                                                                      as we stood
                                                                                at the board?
Remember when we used to iron?

# IN THE WATERS OF MY MOTHER'S PEOPLE

In the waters of my mother's people,
A mermaid rests on a rock.
She looks back to shoreline,
For the ship, her lifeline
In the storm.
The masthead of wood so handsome,
So promising to her,
Whispering in the night
Sweet songs of love.

He does not come.
Sleepless she waits.
There is no other choice.

In the waters of my mother's people
A sailor walks back and forth on the deck
In moonlight, restless too.
Why can't he sleep?
Something in the air,
Vaguely, imperceptibly there,
Whispering as a mist,
Into his ear.
Reminding him,
Prodding him—
But the sounds are shapeless, formless.

Still, someone, something's calling.
Out in the deep.
A Presence.
Somewhere waiting.
Restless, he cannot sleep.
Sleepless, she cannot rest.

# Jo*an* **Bloomgarden**

Joan Bloomgarden's positions as director of the Creative Arts Therapy Program and associate professor at Hofstra University reflect the integration of her life experiences. As a young child looking up at the clouds and the sharp blue sky she was a poet; throughout her childhood and into her youth she was a classical dancer, and as an adult she transitioned to visual expression and then to creative arts therapy. Like many other arts therapists, she explored the creative process from a personal as well as from a professional perspective. Her doctoral dissertation in psychology examined creativity in the average person's life.

Joan first became a classroom teacher, then an art teacher, a board certified registered art therapist, and finally a graduate school educator and certified group counselor. She has worked with children in various settings and adults in psychiatric units, conducted a private practice, and supervised art therapists. Her teaching at Hofstra inspires imaginative thought and expression, and engages students in the creative arts. Her national and international publications, presentations, and travel demonstrate her driving passion for the creative process evident in her poetry and visual art.

Dr. Bloomgarden remains deeply involved in her profession by having served on the Art Therapy Credentials Board and by serving on the editorial review boards of the *Journal of the American Art Therapy Association* and *Research and Intervention: Journal of the National Institute for Trauma and Loss in Children*. After September 11, 2001, she provided crisis care through her work with Project Liberty.

I heard a radio interview with a poet selected to write and read his original poem to celebrate a president's birthday. He explained his creative process and reported how a month before the party the poem was not yet written. He did not go to his desk but took long walks in nature knowing that the poem would come.

Sometimes my creative process begins this way, too. I spend quiet moments convening with my surroundings waiting for something to emerge. Other times I feel tension brewing, with ideas racing through my head. I suspend judgment and wait until I feel ready to work. Then I determine which modality, the visual or the verbal, will satisfy.

Media and technique are central to the visual arts. Both influence my art making process and product. Sometimes media help spark ideas. With collage, clay, and color, my special three "Cs," I become immersed in experimentation and discovery. My initial amorphous feelings eventually become defined in a piece of art. I describe the interplay between the media and me as a dance. I use the visual arts when I want a working partner in my creative process.

I become a poet when I am driven to express something specific. I usually have some beginning in mind. I enjoy writing poetry because the written word satisfies my desire for precision while at the same time it demands creativity. I am challenged to come up with just the right metaphors. I struggle to find not only the language but also the rhythm and sound that will complement my message. In the visual arts, I might be satisfied with a mistake and learn to see value in it or enjoy a mysterious corner not yet complete. In my poetry, on the other hand, I strive to be exact.

I respond differently to my artwork than to my poetry. My poems feel complete except for fine editing. My artwork often seems incomplete, and while I am not judgmental of my creative process, I am critical of my artwork, believing that with practice my pieces will improve. I am much more accepting of my poetry. I do not burden it with the expectations I place upon myself as a visual artist.

*Organic* by Joan Bloomgarden
Watercolor, 18" x 24"

## SNOW

I reach for my high boots, my coat, and scarf
And get ready with quiet preparation
So as not to disturb the gentle snowdrifts.
I do not take the shovel sleeping against the house
Nor the brush
But I take my soft stride
And move the snow with my feet
As I walk among the settled flakes
None of them the same.

# Mildred
# Lachman Chapin

Mildred Lachman Chapin has been a painter and art therapist for many decades. Her academic background includes a bachelor's degree from the University of Pennsylvania, where she graduated *cum laude* in economics, and a master's from American University in Washington, D.C. in special education. She has exhibited her paintings abroad and in the United States in museums, public buildings, and galleries. Her 1994 published book, *Reverberations: Mothers and Daughters,* contains her paintings, prints, and poetry.

For the past thirty years, Chapin has been a major contributor to the field of art and art therapy, respected for her numerous articles published in professional journals, and frequent presentations and workshops at national conferences. She is an outstanding scholar and educator who has taught at the Art Institute of Chicago, George Washington University, Vermont College, and the Chicago Psychoanalytic Institute.

In recent years, Millie has exhibited groups of paintings in galleries, often accompanied by related poetry. Some of these series are: "Sisters-in-Spirit" and "Pairs" exhibited in Chicago; "Time, Light, and Stillness," "Calligraphic Impulses," and "Visual Haikus" exhibited in various venues in Arizona.

Presently living in Tucson, she has lived for at least two years each in Italy, Turkey, and France, is quite fluent in French and somewhat in Italian.

Several years ago, I wrote about a series of my paintings. The writing turned out to be poetry. Since I had had little knowledge about poetic literature and technique, I began to study poetry-making. I wondered if I could write poetry not related to paintings, and if so, what would be my source and process.

In both the process and the finished product in each art form, I have a different way of knowing. In poetry writing, I think I know what I am trying to say. New meanings or ideas may come as I am writing, but they come as enrichments to the main thrust. Perhaps because I don't yet have the freedom to explore in poetry, I can't yet play as I can in painting, to create an atmosphere, to leave the reader spinning in a mystery of meaning. I usually don't begin knowing what I mean to say in my painting; it evolves. I may start with a line, a color, a form, or an image I see or imagine. In the finished piece, the image may disappear or be completely changed.

So time is an element to explore. Painting reverberates through time; meaning unfolds to me as I work. I experience differing feelings during the construction of a painting, and it may take a long time to finish. The sustaining feeling may be vaguely persistent, but after many metamorphoses, the finished piece may surprise me. It can reveal more about what I meant, or a viewer can throw light on a meaning I hadn't intended. The poem, by contrast, comes quickly. It may take

months to refine, but its meaning begins to emerge and shine as I polish it. There is not as much surprise or discovery as when I look at my finished painting. The poem feels more finite: I've said it; it's there.

Each medium provides different ways of tapping into my feelings. In poetry, the feeling has to make sense. This requires of me an intermediary step, a kind of censoring—to put into words the ineffable. Painting provides me with more direct access to my feelings. This may be because I have spent decades painting and only a few years at poetry-making, but I think there is something inherently different in these two media, each expressing different levels of experience.

Poetry, for me, is closer to awareness. It gives me comfort to know that its ideas, thoughts, and stories are readily accessible to my language-speaking fellow humans. I have no such comfort with my paintings. They tap more easily into the unconscious, the primal emotions and experiences of our pre-verbal lives and dream worlds. I struggle to form the work knowing that others may not understand. As I attempt to be both poet and painter, I hope my two art forms will complement one another.

*Consoling I* by Mildred Lachman Chapin
Oil on canvas, 29" x 36"

# CONSOLE

She consoles the aging mother,
The mentor left behind in flight to sexual awakening,
The once beauteous queen of all that sheltered and fed,
She who enveloped the girl with import,
Shaped her personhood,
At hand for life-and-death caring,
Emergency service for whatever terrors.

*Don't sorrow for me.*
*I'm off to dance with danger.*
*Sorrow for yourself.*
*Grieve for losing me.*

*Grieve for my emergent beauty*
*Once yours*
*My lust for pleasure, my surprise*
*At how my body vibrates like a plucked harp.*
*Is this, once yours, what you wanted me to have?*
*Is this, once yours, what you feared for me to know?*
*A secret, now for grieving?*

*Your body, mine once for the asking*
*Now dries and wrinkles.*
*Your dancer spring, once sure*
*Is cautious now.*

*You slowly creep to death*
*To lose me once again.*
*All that once was yours will go:*
> *what you see in me*
> *what you used to be.*

*It's my turn now to grieve.*
*Mama! Console me!*

*All the pains of womanhood we both know now*
*Diminish as I think of losing you.*
*No more the matrix of my life adventure*
*You'll leave me for my solo flight.*
*Tell me, mama, you'll kiss and make it better*
*When it happens*

# WE CAN MOURN TOGETHER, MOTHER

We can mourn together, mother.
I too am a wise old woman now, no longer the child, cringing,
        frightened, feeling abandoned by you, your contorted face
        screaming, crying.
You who left me, forgot me. You stood as if alone on a
        windy winter corner on an early Sunday morning,
        sucking on your grief like an ice cream cone.
No one was there but me, watching. What could I do?
        You had left me.
I could never be your ice cream cone. And I had nothing to
        suck on.
Reverberations of images through time now bring me to you,
        resonating with your grief.

# Mary **Davies Cole**

Mary Davies Cole is an artist and board certified, registered art therapist in northern New Jersey. As a licensed professional counselor and professional coach for adults with attention deficit and attention deficit hyperactivity and other disorders, she works with a wide variety of clients in a number of different modalities. Using Art Process Coaching©, a long distance coaching relationship that incorporates artwork, poetry, and other creative media via mail, telephone, and the internet, Mary has worked with clients in several states. Her focus in her private practice in Madison, N.J. is on helping people integrate their personal, professional, and spiritual lives in a way that fosters awareness, growth, and creativity.

Mary holds bachelor's and master's degrees in English literature from Drew University, and a master's in art therapy and creativity development, with distinction, from Pratt Institute. She is also a graduate of Coaches Training Institute in San Rafael, California. On the faculty of the Pratt Graduate Creative Arts Therapy Department for nine years, she is currently teaching at the School of Visual Arts in New York City.

Mary has had a life-long love of poetry and art, and was invited in 1998 to be a speaker at the Rockefeller Foundation's "keyword" conference. She has also participated in the poetry division of the Iowa Writer's Workshop. As an artist, she prefers working in acrylics and pastels. She lives with her husband, Don, and their golden retriever, China.

Robert Frost said once that writing poetry was like "riding easy in harness." I like this. Frost's words conjure up images of rhythm and balance; galloping when energy is high, and cantering when you want the ride to be peaceable.

Riding suggests possession of your own energy, having comfortable control over the message. Not that I always know what the message is; I almost never do when I begin. It knows and presses itself through me, rocking in my body until it finds its way free. Perhaps I find myself writing a journal entry in the form of a poem; the poem doesn't write itself, but it presents itself to be written. I know when the word, the phrase, the color and stroke of the language is mine, even if I am not sure what the completed poem will say to me or to someone else. My images—visual or verbal—visit me; as I find expression for them, I find what I like to call, the "true line."

My true line emerges in times of intensity: The death of my mother comes to mind and the birth of my sons. In such moments I am driven to expression, snapped to attention by an invisible force, impossible to ignore. The line dances itself into being, sometimes direct, sometimes sly. In this way, images present themselves demanding discharge. Sometimes these energies are elusive, arbitrary, maddeningly absent when ardently desired, bountifully present when I am least prepared.

I write or paint until the main idea is there. Then, as often as not, I put the poem or artwork away. Later, making contact with the image from a distance, I put on the harness. When I edit a poem or rework a drawing, its meaning brightens, becomes clearer. The message is awakened by intention and focus.

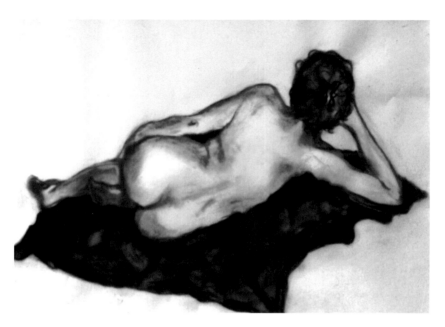

*Silence* by Mary Davies Cole
Pencil on paper, 14" x 18"

# LEAVING IT TO THE BREEZE

Hanging out the wash
A mere physical thing,
Pin after pin,
Extending myself to the limit of the line.
Simple, like doing what you have to do,
Leaving it to the breeze.

I'll take it in, dry and bright,
Smell of the wind on my fingertips,
Stiff with the smart crease of
The all-outdoors, the flags that waved hello
All day long, later today.

Wish I could hang out there myself,
Naked as a leaf
And just as ordinary,
Veined and plain—
Shake out this shell and fill her up
With new breath: my wind-whipped chance,
My holy communion with the air,
Homely ritual to remind myself
Where things stand:
Laundry/enlightenment.

## SONG AT MY MOTHER'S DEATH

Clouded silence is in charge today    melon colored like the evening sun,
                         it smells of salt.
Ribbons of rain cord heaven            with this empty earth
                    the waiting
                    the waiting
breath breathes heavy      skin too small      some part escapes/leaps frantic
beats its wings against the windowpanes      collapses back and curls inside itself
                    but cannot sleep.


Is this the final separation, then      flesh from flesh,
one spirit                              from another here?
Woman whom I've railed against      (and loved)
you      original blood-nest of strangled hopes unwearied fears
I hold them now   cold and fierce                swallow them whole
declare them mine                      at last.
But what of yours            what do you carry into this last shade?
Fingers of time draw your dreams out of my eyes like wild swans
lusts and loves                  forgotten
the song of the body self unsung:
                    sweetness of nectar
                    lightness of light
                    sing now, into night.

# NIGHT FLIGHT IN OCTOBER

O moon, October moon,
I lie down naked in your womblike light.
Corn poppies bow
In the presence of a shrine,
An altar of pear trees, the gentle service of the wind.
For so long I was a woman
In search of a woman who seeks herself,
Like a painter attempting self-portrait
In a mirror's absence.
Tonight, sister Earth holds up my body,
Only itself, grass for bed, clouds for cover,
The kiss of the warm Autumn dark.
I hold nothing in my hands;
My limbs lie forgotten in the meadow;
My eyes you keep steady upon yourself—
I have nothing to offer.
By what alchemy do I become moon?
Soaring in my own light I spread across the land
In ethers of another time. Steeples rise in me,
I flood the dreams of sleepers,
Enter boldly the corners of lovers,
Pass through their sighs back out into the night.
I bless the wanderer. She calls me, "Mother."
The sounds of dark slip through the air,
Travel before me in muted landscapes.
Hawk swoops down; owl calls out
For who is there. Rivers go on rushing, and only the beasts
Know their pulse. Deer move like dancers,
Rabbits graze in clover field.
I cast myself across the waters,
Ride stallion waves to ancient shores,
Lick cracked crabshell,
Seashells, blown bottles pitted deep,
Crawling snail. On countless particles of sand
I glitter for a second, and sweep away.
Fishermen come; the dawn curves into sight.
Gathering my beams about me,
I travel homeward until I see,
Lying there upon the meadow grass,
The still and breathless body of a woman
Who believes she dreams.

# *Carol* **Thayer Cox**

Having grown up on the Jersey shore, Carol Thayer Cox moved to Virginia to attend school, found the man of her dreams, and decided to stay. She graduated in 1968 with a bachelor's in art history from Mary Washington College of the University of Virginia. During the 1970's, she co-owned an art gallery and framing shop and then went back to school and earned her master's in art therapy from George Washington University in 1984.

For ten years Carol was assistant director of the graduate art therapy program of George Washington University, was on the faculty of Vermont College's art therapy program for five years, and continues to lecture at a number of institutions and national conferences. A long-time devotee of Carl Jung's work and a certified instructor of the MARI® Course in Mandala Assessment for close to 20 years, she has taught internationally on color, imagery, and symbolism across the life cycle. She founded *MUSE*, a performing arts troupe, that teaches psychological theory through art, dance, music, and poetry. Carol currently has a part-time private practice in Washington, D.C. where she supervises art therapists and other clinicians whose patients make art.

Carol's writing has been published in professional book chapters and journal articles. She is co-author with Barry Cohen of *Telling Without Talking: A Window into the World of Multiple Personality*. Cohen and Cox are currently working on a new book about understanding abstract art.

Having spent many years helping to raise her two children and seven stepchildren, Carol is enjoying spending time with her retired husband Jerry in their home in the quiet Virginia countryside. Now that she has her own studio, she looks forward to making art again—mixed media collages, woodcuts, and paintings—and she hopes to show her work regionally as she has done before.

Before making art or poetry, I feel tension—a pressing need to create. This tension is elicited by a particular experience of seeing, hearing, touching, or remembering that causes a sense of longing in me.

The images, sounds, and colors percolate inside, waiting for expression. My unconscious mind slowly synthesizes the experience, providing a framework for these sensory or intuitive fragments in order to manifest meaning.

I first encountered this process when I was in college and was grappling with a theorem that no one in my logic class had been able to solve. It was a conundrum, a challenge I had doggedly pursued. When I came home for semester break, however, I promptly forgot about it. One day, while thinking about something totally different, I was suddenly struck with the correct way to prove the theorem. It was a complex and creative answer that my mind had apparently been working on without my conscious awareness.

Poems and paintings have come to me in similar ways—not always so dramatically, but often enough to make me a believer in this cauldron of creativity that lurks below the surface. Much of my creative process occurs silently within. It keeps me company on long drives and sleepless nights. I count on its being there when I'm finally ready. Sometimes I don't tend to it soon enough. A previously passionate voice can lose its intensity once I have pen in hand, and a visual image depicted beautifully in my imagination can dissipate once I've prepared the canvas. Forcing a creation out prematurely can have unsatisfactory results as well. Recognizing the optimum moment to create is key.

I've come to trust in this incubation phase of the creative process that requires little conscious input from me other than honoring the inspiration, tending the fire, holding the tension, and setting the stage for eventual birth. If I allow enough time for incubation, an architecture begins to take form.

When I can respond in a timely manner and decide to write poetry, it is usually because words have already begun to define the experience for me. I enter a space of deep silence where I can listen to sounds and rhythms as they come together to convey meaning. Being immersed in this process extends the tension and perpetuates the longing. My knowledge of the rules of language facilitates the unconscious creation of structure that will hold the poem together.

When I respond by going to my studio, it's because there are no words. The images and feelings are haunting; they demand to be rendered visual. The process of making shape, color, and texture and combining them into something meaningful often awakens a new sense of longing, recapitulating my initial moment of inspiration. My understanding of composition supports the unconscious transformation that makes form out of formlessness.

Only with great sadness do I ignore the muse who tells me when it is time to pick up the paintbrush or pen.

*Rosescape* by Carol Thayer Cox
Acrylic on canvas, 24" x 24"

# BEYOND BLUE VIOLET

Today
we went
beyond
blue violet
into the familiar
and the unfamiliar
where we touched
at the still point

sustaining
the vibration
of our prayer
as we danced
in stillness a
dance that
took us
through
centuries
of space
and time

feeling the vastness
separating us and
connecting us
we wept
with
joy
and
sorrow
on the threshold
of understanding

# REFINISHING

Stripping layers of paint down to bare rough wood,
sanding in sweltering heat while blistering my
hands to return this heirloom to its once
smooth surface, I drift into reverie
with the rhythm and hum
this old bed holds.

Transported by my task to a century before,
I become the carpenter who chose the
lumber, sawed the boards, turned
the wood, matched the grain,
joined the parts, lovingly
crafting and finishing
this bed to last.

Buffing the headboard to a silken touch,
I wonder what dreams this bed could
tell: what songs it could sing, what
laughter it has heard, what tears
it has tasted. Rubbing in stain
to a velvety blush, I think
of the growing pains
this bed has felt..

Varnishing bedposts worn uneven from
years of being touched by the young
hands of my mother, then those of
my daughter, I am grateful this
bed had cradled them both so
well. Now the elder is gone
and the younger is grown;
memories remain with
this bed and me.

# UNEXPRESSIONS

What happens to unspoken words?
Once thought, they seem alive
enough inside of me.
I can sometimes hear
sounds of the syllables
being formed, as if I had actually
said them out loud.
But when I did not, where did they go?

That dance I choreographed
to echoes of the wind...
I envisioned each step
and practiced within my mind
motions of the sea.
But I never let my dance
move in space outside of me.
What becomes of undanced dances?

What about the painting
that never got the brushes wet?
I could sense the texture
and see the smoothness
of each color I applied
as the images began to form
on that imaginary canvas.
Is there a gallery for these works?

The other day I thought of a song
inspired by a friend's words:
"Always on the edge of tears."
I loved the minor key
chorus I composed
but never gave it voice.
Is there a place for unsung songs?
Are they like uncried tears?

Are these on the edge creations
like abortions—thwarted
in their beginnings?
Once thought or felt,
do they have their own energy
to survive until found again,
or will they die
for want of sound or movement?

Perhaps like messages in bottles,
they are cryptic
reminders of creative sparks
encapsulated too soon,
thrown into the surging
rhythm of my life,
where one day they will resurface,
to be expressed at last.

# Ellen **Roth Deutsch**

Ellen Roth Deutsch grew up in New York City during the 1940s and '50s in an artistic family. Her father and three uncles were nationally syndicated cartoonists known as the Four Roth Brothers. As a child she received instruction from her father and attended classes at the Art Students League. Deutsch was also interested in science and obtained a bachelor's degree in biology and chemistry from the City College of New York in 1961 and a master's in microbiology from North Carolina State University in 1976. She worked in the Genetics and Metabolism Laboratory at the University of Illinois Hospital doing research and clinical work, and as a consultant for Abbott Labs.

Influenced by musicals and theater in New York during her growing up years, Ellen's artwork is narrative and largely based on her own history. Her paintings and drawings are included in the collections of the James R. Thompson Center, Chicago; the McDonalds Corporation; the Uncle Fun Foundation; and many others, both public and private. Her artwork is included in *The Best of Colored Pencil 4,* published by Rockport in 1997.

Ms. Deutsch's limited edition book, *Mr. Swift and the Brown Shoes,* was produced during residencies at Artists Book Works, Chicago, and the Ragdale Foundation and is available in the library collections of the School of the Art Institute of Chicago, the Museum of Contemporary Art, Chicago, and the National Museum of Women in the Arts, Washington, D.C. In 1996, her poem, "A Memory About Language" was included in *Poetry for Peace,* published by the Peace Museum of Chicago. Her artist's books incorporate text along with visual imagery.

"A Memory About Language" is based on an actual incident that occurred in 1950 in the bungalow colony her parents and aunts and uncles owned in the Catskill Mountains in New York.

Most of my work, visual art and poetry, derives from personal experience and feelings. Through the work I am telling my own and other women's stories.

I have dealt with such different subjects as growing up in New York City during the 1940s and '50s, the roles of girls and women in fairy tales, childhood sexual abuse and molestation, and presently, the survival of the spirit.

My work, in general, contains a recurrent theme of bondage and entrapment. I use threads, vines, bandages, wrappings, and spider webs to envelop my images of people and symbolize their connection to the roles they play within their culture or relationships, and to their histories. In the drawings for "A Memory About Language," I used the image of barbed wire to recall the concentration camps, since the holocaust survivors were forever bound to their past.

First thing in the morning, my images and ideas flow easily. I am disciplined about working, starting early and working five to six hours, whether I'm feeling creative or not. Just starting helps. If I'm not feeling creative, I read other people's work or go to galleries to get my juices flowing.

I usually create artwork as a series on a specific theme, often spanning a number of years. I have worked in different media depending on the topic. The subject defines the medium. I sharpen up the visual work continuously as I go along, emphasizing key areas.

I write poetry from a strong feeling about an issue or memory that I need to express. I do a lot of editing. I keep going over it, reading it aloud, to get economy of words and reduce the poem to its essence. I pay special attention to the meter or beat and like to use repetition of key phrases.

The creative process for both visual art and poetry seems to be similar. In both cases, I start off somewhere in the middle with a focal point or image that carries an impact, and I develop the piece from there. In time, the work itself takes over and dictates the next step. I have to give up any preconceptions about what the work should look like. I'm in another state of mind, a suspended state where words and visuals come freely. My strongest and best work results from letting go and trusting my instincts.

*A Memory of Language* by Ellen Roth Deutsch
Prismacolor drawing from artist's book, page 8, 6" x 5"

# A MEMORY ABOUT LANGUAGE,

IN 1950, WHEN I WAS NINE
WE LIVED ON A LAKE IN THE CATSKILL MOUNTAINS,
RENTING COOL AIR AND WATER TO CITY PEOPLE
FLEEING THE CONCRETE SUMMER HEAT.

THEN, THE NIGHT SKY WAS CROWDED WITH STARS,
THE ONLY AIR TRAFFIC FROM BEES, GNATS AND
BUTTERFLIES SHARING SPACE
AROUND WHITE ROSE - FILLED TRELLISES.

CYD AND FRED DANCED, ESTHER SWAM,
AND DOROTHY WENT TO OZ,
WHILE WE CHILDREN SPLASHED AND RAN,
FILLING BUCKETS WITH BLUEBERRIES AND TADPOLES.

TWO FAMILIES CAME THAT YEAR,
WITH THREE CHILDREN
AND A BABY NAMED IRVING,
BLUE NUMBERS TATTOOED ON THEIR ARMS.

THEY SPOKE IN A TONGUE FAMILIAR
BUT NOT UNDERSTOOD,
REMINISCENT OF CONVERSATIONS AMONG GRANDPARENTS
AROUND TABLES FILLED WITH FOOD.

STANDING AT THE EDGE OF THE SHIMMERING GRAY WATER
THEY BREATHED IN AIR MADE FRAGRANT BY LILACS
AND COOLED BY TALL TREES,
THE OLDEST RESIDENTS OF OUR COLONY.

ON A HOUSE TOP NEARBY
A WEATHER VANE CREAKED
MOVED BY A RUSH OF SUMMER WIND.

LOOKING UP, THEIR FRAGILE FACES SHATTERED WITH FEAR
BY A GLIMPSE OF THE BLACK IMAGE;
REMEMBERING PAIN, SOULS LOST,
SMELLS OF DEATH AND CAMPS OF ASHES.

SOUNDS FROM THEIR RAPID TONGUES FILLED THE AIR
AS THEY FOUGHT TO STAY IN 1950.
OUR PARENTS ACCOMMODATED AND SOOTHED
IN ORDER TO KEEP THEM THERE.

THAT SUMMER,
THEIR CHILDREN JOINED US IN PLAY.

WE TAUGHT THEM BASEBALL AND JUMP ROPE,
"MONOPOLY" AND ENGLISH.
THEY TAUGHT US HISTORY AND YIDDISH
AND THE MILES WERE BRIDGED.

ICH GLAICH DIR (I LIKE YOU)
ICH GLAICH DIR NICHT (I DON'T LIKE YOU)

ICH BIN FAR-LIHBT MIT DIR (I AM IN LOVE WITH YOU)
ICH BIN FAR-LIHBT MIT DIR NICHT (I AM NOT IN LOVE WITH YOU)

THERE WAS MORE BUT THIS IS ALL I REMEMBER.

ON THE 4TH OF JULY WE STOOD TOGETHER
ON THE PORCH OF THE OLD RED HOUSE,
WATCHING LIGHT AND COLOR EXPLODE
IN REMEMBERANCE OF AN OLDER WAR.

EATING HOTDOGS AND SAUERKRAUT
THEY LAUGHED TO BE THERE.
BUT I DON'T THINK THEY EVER FELT SAFE.

MAYBE IRVING WOULD.

# Joseph C. Di Bella

Joseph C. Di Bella is distinguished professor of art and former chair of the Department of Art and Art History at the University of Mary Washington in Fredericksburg, Virginia, where he has taught since 1977. There he was instrumental in the development of the gallery program and served as director of College Galleries. A recipient of the Grellet Simpson Award for Excellence in Undergraduate Teaching, his specialties are drawing, painting, and color theory. After graduation from Rutgers University, he received his master's and master of fine arts degrees in painting from Northern Illinois University.

A signature member of the National Watercolor Society, a member of the Society of Tempera Painters, and the Phoenix Gallery in New York, Joe has exhibited in international, national, and regional venues both competitive and invitational. His work has received several awards and has been represented in *Best in Watercolor: Painting Color* (Rockport Press, 1997), *Watercolor Expressions* (North Light), and *American Artist*. His drawings illustrate *Home is Another Country* (Mary Washington College Press) by Dan Dervin. Since 2001, Joe's work has been featured in more than a dozen major group and solo exhibitions. He won first place in the National Juried Competition at New York's Phoenix Gallery. Each summer, as co-director of the Mary Washington Program in Urbino, Italy, he visits his favorite places where he teaches, paints, and writes. Along with poetry, opera—particularly of the Italian variety—prompts his muse.

What ties together the making of art and poems? In my experience, the processes share similar qualities. Both place in the palm of the left hand what can be described and represented. Held in the right palm is what can be sensed and intuited.

The hands close around the medium of word or paint to grasp and yield form.

The art process begins with the immediacy of materials and a distance in images. Paint is fluid, liquid, and manipulable. Materials imbue objectivity to the artwork; that is, they make surfaces and spaces. This is where technique plays into the process. Exploring the material aspect of the art process is enjoyable but I am not satisfied with the notion of autonomy of the object. For me, a work of art is to be something that transcends the object. It must induce dialogue. Images carry visual presence and thought weight. My definition of image is broad. In fact, my paintings often employ words as images. Juxtaposing images calls up hybrids of meanings. Ambiguities can arise when seemingly known images are juxtaposed to create unfamiliar image groups. The configuration or confluence of images into visual phrases and pattern produces form which signifies something beyond the images themselves. Analogies can then unfold in the tense tug between the layers of material, image, and form.

For me, the poetry process begins with the need to express when prompted by something seen or read. To that extent, the stimulus is an external one. The nature of word language provides both possibilities and limitations of expression. I begin with the intention of exact definition. Yet exhaustive precision can be stupefying in the poetic process. When words group with other words, meanings emerge, coalesce, and collide. Grouping pulls away from exactness. Word groups give space, shape, visual allusion, and subtlety to images and ideas that hide inchoate and dormant in my mind. Recurrent sounds and rhythmic syllabic divisions are the near tangible qualities of words that accompany their thought weight. Poetry's purpose for me is to heighten awareness of what is missing and not what is evident.

Paintings and poems are deceivingly compact as though somehow their mass is neatly and measurably contained in their packages. They really are much larger. In their supposed concrete finiteness—brush strokes on canvas, characters on paper—they prompt us to consider what we really can know about the vastness of existence. Knowing, in fact, is the ongoing act of thumbing through their layers.

*Amaranth and Suspended Time* by Joseph Di Bella
Watercolor monotype, 22" x 30"

## FIVE MEASURES TO MEANING

The anxious hands of painter
            who would be writer.

Alone.   Listening.

Paper mark.   Paper word.

The difference is the medium.

Not true: deceptive devices.


## DIALOGUE

My muse,
dimpled darling carrot head
of orange peel curves
bent dry and convulsed,
why do you labor?


Will you be delivered
as a woman pregnant
in her tenth month
whose only want is rid?
Then what would waiting be?


You volley your thoughts
and return them
like flapjacks tossed
by a wary cook
whose only task is practice.

## RALLENTANDO IN SPRING: TO KIEFER AND ELIOT

Harrowed field:
        its first cuts bleed brown dirt
        from encrusted skin beneath
        a shroud, its burial cloth
        the sanctified white of winter.

And now it breeds brown worms:
        untied threads from their epidermal cloth
        woof and warp the slender lines
        one to another in the softened, buoyant loam
        of early April.

Here lie men:
        beneath the emerald canopy
        that sheltered friends and family
        from the rain that cruelest day.
        Your golden hair, your white cast bones.

# Audrey **Di Maria**

Audrey Di Maria earned her bachelor's degree in English from Keene State College in New Hampshire and her master's in art therapy at George Washington University in Washington, D.C. She has worked for more than 25 years as an art therapist with emotionally disturbed children at the Paul Robeson School for Growth and Development, a psychoeducational facility operated by the District of Columbia Department of Mental Health. In 1997, she was given the American Art Therapy Association's Clinician Award for her work. She is adjunct associate professor of art therapy at George Washington University.

As a member of the American Art Therapy Association, Audrey has chaired the education committee, a subcommittee on art therapy in the schools, and the publications committee for which she served as editor-in-chief or co-editor of several conference proceedings. She was secretary of the Art Therapy Credentials Board. In 2001, Di Maria was invited to present testimony on art therapy training and credentialing for the White House Commission on Complementary and Alternative Medicine Policy.

A community activist as well, Ms. Di Maria has developed and coordinated exhibits for the U.S. Department of Health and Human Services, the D.C. Government Commission on Mental Health Services, and the D.C. Commission on Social Services to showcase the artwork of people in treatment for emotional disorders.

Audrey is a dedicated member of the "Levy and Fishman Watercolor Group," which has met biweekly since its inception in 1984. She enjoys documenting her world travel with her photography.

It seems as though I have written for as long as I can remember. A dear aunt recalls having rebuked me, at age eight, for wasting "good money" on the ticket she had bought me to see the Ringling Brothers, Barnum and Bailey Circus.

Her impression was that I'd sat through it with my nose in a notebook, my fingers working away. She remembers having torn the pad from my grasp in anger, only to find, when she inspected it days later, that the pages were awash with descriptions of what had been going on simultaneously in all three rings. I spent my latency observing, containing, categorizing—and silently defending the right to do so.

As I alternately surged and limped into adolescence, churning emotions seemed to find their way down my arm and into a pen, to land with a splat on paper where they could be viewed, like animals in a cage, or simply shut safely away. Getting them down and out brought satisfaction born of relief and, if I were lucky, a nugget of understanding. My journals were holding environments. That the process worked, with only paper, pen, and what I brought to it, amazed me. It seemed magical.

While turbulence often provided the catalyst for the tumbling forth of word pictures, paintings grew out of more quiet spaces. The process engendered by picking up a brush stilled my mind, allowing me to look more closely, more deeply. As my eyes focused upon an image, my mind would wrap itself around it, caressing it, weighing it, tasting it. Via my brush, I'd slide down its folds, feel my way through its shadows, reach for its peaks. Light would shimmer and dim as I negotiated my way around it. At times, like a mantra, the focus would flicker and fade, turning the process of painting into a treasure hunt. Yet often, the canvas seemed to paint itself, surprising me by what had taken place, seemingly in my absence.

As an art therapist, I fervently believe that each of us has a well of creativity into which we may dip, once we discover our divining rod. I was fortunate, from an early age, to have been supported by my mother, a teacher of both English and art, who hung my artistic daubings and scrawlings on the refrigerator door and saved all of my stories. Later, I was the student of Bernard Levy, the founder of the George Washington University Art Therapy Program and instructor of watercolor painting, who similarly encouraged my artistic efforts by helping me to expand my palette, loosen my grip, and view apparent mistakes as acts of God. Whether I am painting, writing, or practicing art therapy, I strive to keep their legacies alive.

*On the Isle of Mull (Scotland)* by Audrey Di Maria
Watercolor, 22" x 33"

## UPON STARTING ANALYSIS – September, 1979

Analysis is starting...and continuing.

A rainy Monday
    Up at 6 to pull myself together
       to take myself apart

Rushing up Mass. Ave. to Wisconsin
Rain slapping my window
Anticipation slapping my calm

Do I want this?
Do I need this?
Why am I doing this?

Am I jumping again?
Jumping over anxiety,
Jumping over thought.

But, this time, thought lies on the other side.
    I don't expect a soft landing.

The rain continues.
I find myself inside.
    In...side.

What do I feel?
A fear of flooding, I respond.
I feel a fear of flooding.

Not that my container will break,
But that it won't be able to hold what wells up inside of it.

Perhaps I'll at least come to know what it is that's welling up.
And, perhaps, my container will grow.

# Mimi **Farrelly**

Born and raised in rural northern New Jersey, Mimi Farrelly graduated from Noroton School in Connecticut and earned her undergraduate degree in art history from Smith College. She has master's degrees from Columbia University in early childhood education and from Vermont College of Norwich University in art therapy.

Mimi is the founder, former director, and recently retired adjunct faculty member of the Graduate Art Therapy and Transpersonal Counseling Program at Naropa University in Boulder, Colorado. A founding member of the Colorado Art Therapy Association, she later received its Above and Beyond Award. For over 25 years Mimi has provided art therapy services for sexually abused clients, transculturally and/or transracially adopted children, persons with persistent brain disorders and participants in spiritual growth retreats and workshops.

As a writer, Mimi is editor of *Spirituality and Art Therapy: Living the Connection.* Her included chapter, "Nature: Art Therapy in Partnership with the Earth," describes Mimi's innovative work, as does her chapter in the book, *Creative Art Therapy Approaches in Adoption and Foster Care.* A member of the Columbine Poets of Colorado, her poem "Double Image" is published in their anthology *The Silver Lode.*

Mimi's artwork has been presented in juried solo and group exhibits throughout Colorado. Painter, poet, printmaker, wife, mother, and teacher, she manages to be active in community service. When she is not working, Mimi replenishes her energy performing with a liturgical dance group, gardening, and hiking.

Visual art and poetry—both call me to the witness stand; both challenge me to stop, look, listen; both take seed in attending to inner and outer landscape; both invite me into mystery and awe.

Growing up with poetry read aloud, poetry memorized and recited, poetry written, I learned to savor words beautifully spoken and arranged, images skillfully suggested and juxtaposed. Making visual art came later, when in my twenties I had abandoned poetry and could not find adequately raw speech for mounting confusion and pain. Now I speak both languages, in phases, switching back and forth at irregular intervals.

In a general way I could say visual art brings out deeper, often unconscious material. I lose myself in the sheer pleasure of handling media and experimenting with color, line, form, texture, rhythm. The resulting product often startles me with its honest commentary about my current life situation. I keep an art journal, mostly private, although occasional images beg for fuller expression. I also love the intimacy of drawing from life, whether my subject is a dead sparrow, a fully bloomed hyacinth, or a fellow passenger on a train. Lately I have enjoyed making Mylar stencils of certain drawn images, then using them in monoprints, which provide vividly colored and richly textured and layered environments. I like the serial aspect of printmaking, watching an idea grow and change with each reworking of my stencils on the inked plate.

My poetry shares certain formal qualities with my art making: a deep connection to the natural world, a certain restraint of design, and an appreciation for ambiguity and empty space. Overall, it seems more about a mood, more ephemeral. "Twilight Reverie" burst out of me in a moment of appreciation for the glorious late afternoon light on the broom grass and lake just north of our kitchen sink, and for the precious minutes when domestic chores could be set aside. "A Mother's Death – One Year Later" began with the startling realization that the bedroom carpet on which I was doing morning stretches almost duplicated the blue-gray carpet in the room where my mother died the previous summer. "Double Image," another kitchen poem, helped me, and later my husband, make peace with my regular departure into realms aesthetic and imaginal. Poetry extends such moments. As I write and refine and ponder a certain word or phrase, other things open up in my head.

The bottom line for me is energy. Both art forms bring me closer to that nameless, boundless energy in which we all participate. Appreciating the world through visual art and poetry expands my capacity to love.

*Mothergarden I* by Mimi Farrelly
Monoprint, 12" x 16"

# A MOTHER'S DEATH – ONE YEAR LATER

Violet clouds of memory
confound
these days of June,
shawling
the familiar
with
woven then and now.
My daybreak stretch on muted blue,
my room?
or is it yours?
That meadowlark – a whippoorwill?
Who's
welcoming
this dawn?
Paul's roses here;
Dad's roses there.
Pearls in either drawer.
Your room
had
mapled shade
and
chintz;
mine is simpler, unadorned.

# DOUBLE IMAGE – for Paul

*"Art is the only way to run away without leaving home."* —Twyla Tharp

You think you know this kitchen woman,
kneading, mixing, tending stove,
and judging her to be the same as twines
with you sometimes at noon,
you speak mid-morning things:
a speed trap on the Boulder road,
a grocery need, an airplane joke.

But I am not as you have seen,
nod mute from spaces in between,
my spirit flown to cloister cell for holy work
of measuring, sifting words and thoughts,
stirring, boiling, sloughing off
in service of a poet tribe
which also knows my name.

You leave. Rebuked? Or puzzled by the shift?
What signals had you missed?

I turn fresh muffins out to cool,
rinse greens, and settle
on the couch my mother bought me
years ago when she despaired
that any man would have this bride:
more cat than dog,
more hollyhock than rose

Originally published in *The Silver Lode* (2003) by the Columbine Poetry Society

## TWILIGHT REVERIE

This is the magic hour
when a mother's sneakers have stood long enough
at the sink and the stove,
when supper tends itself,
when a child's late nap and the
gap of the evening news
grant reprieve;
when I slip away to the tawny embrace
of an unimproved back yard.

Here is the cocktail I seek!
Late October light, like honey
trickling over pale dry corn.
Steel blue lake rippled by wind and
the bobbing ebullience of diving ducks,
mistaken at first glance for channel markers
in the inland sea
of my waking dream.
How often have I smelled the green Atlantic
on the breeze that bends the broom grass?
or tasted salt marsh and low tide
as with my daughter I drew finger pictures
in the powder–dusted lane?

This view is my sustainer.
Always the mountains, the grasses, the crops.
Always the lake calling…calling.
Like the russet hawk I prey upon its shores,
patient in my freedom to surprise,
not mouse nor vole
but with my eyes to feast
on ever changing subtleties
of sound and hue.

The oven timer rings me back.
Enter a floaty, flirtatious housewife
drunk on twilight liquor,
gratefully renewed.

# Mary-Michola
# Fibich

Mary-Michola Fibich was born in 1964 in beautiful Colorado. She began journal and poetry writing when she was six, drawing and painting soon after. She used her creativity to capture the natural beauty around her and to record and transform her childhood.

Mary decided to become an art therapist after her mother showed her an article about the field. She completed her undergraduate degree at Bowling Green State University where she majored in art therapy and minored in psychology and art. She worked at a state mental health facility for two years before earning her master's degree in art therapy at George Washington University.

Over the years, she worked in many other settings including hospices, nursing homes, a special education school, group homes, and day treatment programs. From 1991-1996, Mary worked at The Center: Post-Traumatic and Dissociative Disorders Program in Washington, D.C. Out of that rewarding and challenging work experience came the book, "Managing Traumatic Stress through Art" (Sidran Press, 1995) which she wrote with two colleagues, Barry M. Cohen and Anita B. Rankin. From 1996-2001, she owned with her mother the consulting company, Trust Works, which focused on human and spiritual development in the workplace. Mary is a published poet and is often commissioned as a watercolor artist.

Mary's creative passion today is invested in being a full-time parent with her husband, Don, to their two young sons, Jack and Will. She currently lives in Orange Park, Florida where she hopes the ocean and tropical landscapes of Florida, like the mountains of Colorado, will inspire more creativity in the years ahead.

Today there are two forces that drive my creative process: a need to manage and a desire to transform. Using creativity to manage my life began when I was twelve years old.

Unexpected losses of a parent through divorce and a friend through murder interrupted my childhood. Art and poetry became holding environments for my responses to these events.

Later in life, I learned that making art and writing poetry could be transformative. Creative works not only commemorate struggles, but also contain new perspectives for which I am grateful, offering solace, strength, and wisdom. Engaging in the creative process allows me to release as well as receive.

Oil painting, collage, drawing, and sculpture reflect some aspect of my life that needs to be addressed and provide me with release. I start with an image and I remain open to whatever comes through me and from me, not always knowing the direction the art will take. Sometimes the artwork tells a story I understand; other times I must wait for clarity to come.

When I paint flowers or landscapes with watercolors, I receive. I am replenished by depicting and recreating beauty in the natural world. Although my spirit usually finds its way to the image, its colors, shapes, and textures, the painting isn't about encounter or expression of self. It is a haven.

Poetry writing provides the same kind of letting go and taking in. The process allows me to release intense feelings and receive my own compassionate response. Recently, when reviewing years of work, I realized that my poems are simply prayers. I say a prayer in the first stanzas where I express concerns, ask questions, review needs, seek support, or recall memorable experiences. The last stanzas provide answers, guidance, and encouragement. Poetry not only concretizes the present, it gives direction and insight for the future.

Whether my need is to release or receive, manage or transform, art and poetry serve me well. I always hope that they can serve others too. Maybe by placing my truths on paper, I can bring others closer to their own truths.

*For Suzanne* by Mary-Michola Fibich
Watercolor and gouache, 9" x 12"

All things have led to this time and place.

Boxed and bagged debris
bury the tracks aimed east.
Whitewashed fences
line the road west.

All the small revolutions
molded me for this moment.
All the years of untying crafty knots
mended me for today.

I ask for help.
Vandals still find their way to these walls.
Gravity still makes it monotone.

All I want is to be hungry
to be handed a torch
to be brave
to accept this bounty.
All I want is a champion.

All I need is permission.

There is no sin in being handed
what I need
what I want.
There is no reward in suffering.

Gather some food and clothes.
Do not go back to what is known.
Someone worked years painting this landscape.
Take and receive.

How pleasing.
Leave the room how you found it.
Leave the room how you found it.
Put everything back where it belongs.
Make the room forget you were there.

Be calm, don't breathe.
Keep quiet.
Better safe than sorry.
Change sounds and shapes
to meet the audience where they settle.
No wonder there is no place to call home.

Old slideshows lit me up today.
Passion cursed me too many nights.
Finally listened, moved and made room.
Still seeking revenge.
Cannot tell a lie.

Thick skin and so small lungs
keep the fire somewhere small.
Heat in history held rage, clouds.
Heat in me holds truth, light.
Start over.
Start over.
Dissolve the pact,
wired to punish,
miscarry.

Watch over me now.
Watch me now.
Will
no longer fight life.
Will
make you proud.
Blueprint once tattooed
washes off with water.
Start over.
Over and over.

Move a chair toward the window, light.
Paint a wall red or yellow, heat.
Straighten a photo on the desk, truth.
Make the room remember you were there.

# Mari **Marks Fleming**

Mari Marks Fleming, a registered art therapist, is board certified and licensed as a marriage and family counselor in California. She worked in residential and hospital settings in the Washington, D.C. area; served on the art therapy faculty of George Washington University (GWU); and consulted to Walter Reed Army Medical Center. Mari has taught in other graduate level programs, principally California State University, Sacramento, and The College of Notre Dame of Belmont, California. She has spoken nationally and published book chapters, papers, and book reviews in the field of art therapy.

Mari received the American Art Therapy Association's Art Therapy Clinicians Award in 1996 for her work with adolescents and families. She served on the Association's nominations committee and on its educational program approval board. She was also chair for regional family art therapy symposia.

In 1975 at GWU, Mari was one of the first students in the country to earn a master's degree in art therapy, having received her bachelor of fine arts in painting with highest honors from the University of Illinois in 1954. Accomplished as an art therapist, Mari is renowned as a fine artist. She paints in encaustics (beeswax and pigments), is included in the 2001 book, *The Art of Encaustic Painting,* by Joanne Mattera, exhibits, and sells her work. She is a recipient of numerous honors. Her work has been shown on both coasts of this country: a solo exhibit at the Dolby Chadwick Gallery in San Francisco, numerous other exhibitions in the Bay Area, New York, and Washington, D.C. Her work is represented in Japan and in the Halle Berry collection, as well as in the collections of Hilton Hotels, Hewlett Packard, the California State Health Department, Alzo Pharmaceuticals, and Mercury Interactive.

Residing in Berkeley, Mari maintains a private practice and lectures. Recently she has taught painting as meditation for Naropa College West. She fills her life with the activities of her concert pianist husband, music, gardening, home, children and grandchildren.

I am a visual artist. And, sometimes, I write. I write out of experience, out of feeling, out of thought. I write while looking or listening, my hand moving, associations rising.

Sometimes it just goes right, and I fall in love with a turn of phrase, a rhythm, the pleasure that this poem has come from me.

The beginnings of painting, the sketches, first lines and colors, first thinking and experiencing with materials, can be like poem making. Art making for me is about the sensation of the making, the materiality, the moment distilled, the interaction cherished. It is not about incident, but about what remains, where the structure informs and co-creates idea.

My poems are out of feeling not distilled—the impulse, the cry, the terrible wish someone would hear. Or I may write out of the need to find meaning, to put into words what I have felt or been. The biggest difference between the writing of poetry and the making of art is in how much I know. Words sing to me their own melody and rhythm out of my intuitive sense of rightness. In poetry I don't make the same demands on myself, the same comparisons with what is and is not "art." Since I don't know the form, or the questions, I can survive my doubts and self-criticism.

In art, I exult in ruthless cutting, slashing at my favorite passages; too pretty must be sacrificed, too easy will obscure the edge of truth. In art I know the form and the questions. The act of painting contains enough experience, enough pleasure, to hold me through the agonies of doubt. Art making comforts me; it holds my distress. Through form I attempt to convey truth.

In my art, I invite truth by repetitions, periodicity, movement of thread, incorporated grasses and leaves. I preserve an exquisite moment in time by portraying the interaction of an image seen and seen again, refracted, reflected. My art is a lens, shifting through layered thought and associations. It deepens the image, acknowledges what cannot be changed or covered over, or in covering over, reveals the truth of the covering.

In my poetry, I write thoughts and feelings into being using words that seek understanding, appear translucent, reveal all. My poetry is linear; it tells a story chronologically. My art, by contrast, is more complex. Its layering of media and images discloses experience as it is transmuted over time. While my writing talks about truth, my art is truth.

*Cycle of the Years, The Fall with Meditations*
by Mari Marks Fleming
Mixed media, oil, and beeswax on board, 80" x 48" x 9"

## THOUGHTS ON MUSIC
## AT THE BERKELEY STORE GALLERY

It's a cold night.
December, and we're all alone and it gets colder.
March will be hell this year.

Think about music.

Textures, colors, and, of course, rhythm
Cast out in air,
Or grabbed and brought back home,
Caressed, set side by side, polished,
Unique each one.
Jammed all together. Crashed. Smashed.
Swept up clean.
A note rolls across and teeters
Drawing out the line on point.

Circle round a note forgotten.
Describe its volume, tone and timbre.
Cut shards of memory in dark let fall.
Rub the echoes till they glow.

Music reaches inside, takes dimension of rib cage,
Hones the surgeon's knife,
Cuts clean, describing all the edges,
Planes the curve of muscles, plucks ligaments,
Takes up being in the space vibration carves.

And vibration moves, itself a wave.
Yet is itself no thing.
Only something where it touches and is not.
And in the space between,
A something that touches shore in me.

# FROM THE BOOK ABOUT HIDING

How do I hide?
I hide as I think about and not be.
I hide in corners and out in the open
Still as a chair.
I hide while being not me.

Hiding. To hide. An active verb.
Someone does the hiding.
Which implies someone will be looking.

There are no signs.
But follow the clues, watch for the trail, discover the secret map—
Encoded mystic marks, the private language, notations,
Reminders of secret thought, the jog to memory.
Is hiding a way of making active
     never being seen?

Once I, this, was hidden there.
Just now, I am prepared to hide, secrete away,
Some thing.
Put in a place specific, away from sight, cover over, mask, obscure the traces,
Forget.
But even if it's never found, somehow the area must be marked off,
Boundaries extended.
And even farther, make the boundary
Hit the mark like every other mark so nothing is hidden.

If one moment there is nothing where a minute before
There was a continuous space,
Will you be curious where erasure leaves white page?
Will you seek the faintest traces, signs of what was there,
As I seek to discover reason in two right turns that keep the same direction?

The clearing where tornado passed?
The break in river flow where water breaks or spreads to turn in a wide arc?
Planes are gone and leave no mark. Silent travelers.
Yet after, the sound travels.

Truth casts a shadow
Whose marks are evidence, whose sounds are visible, whose smell is
    not disguised.
I am free to make the worst, the ugliest, nastiest,
Most empty stuff in the world.
Barriers have always meant protection.

Shall I put up the lights, signal files, flags and bells,
Whistles sounding KEEP OFF?
Venture too close at your peril;
Not mine.

What if I wish to welcome,
Wait for silks and teas from China, for provisions sent to feed
A starving town?
Do we speak the same language?

Hold me in your mantle,
Protect and keep me from the dark.
My body is an ache of sweet remembering.
Hiding can be like that,
Nurturing and enfolding,
Embracing with soft fingers.

I have a hundred fences:
Barbed wire, hedges, trimmed and untrimmed.
A boggy stream, rivers, swamp that fills the track, dust that blows and covers,
Fog. Rank growth.
The ground fallen away. Danger and no sign to warn.
A mirror, inviting, the glass a silvered screen.

I trust my dreams more than remembrance,
The dark more than dreams.

# Pierre A. Grégoire

Pierre A. Grégoire has pursued his interests in psychology, psychology of art, and the therapeutic aspects of the creative arts along with his assignments as part-time faculty in the Fine Arts Department at Concordia University. For over thirty years he has provided teaching, thesis supervision, and research in the Art Education Program, which with his contribution, later expanded into the Creative Arts Therapy Program. Pierre graduated with a doctorate in clinical psychology from the Université de Montréal in 1969 and worked as clinical psychologist and psychotherapist in a university hospital. He is on the faculty of the departments of psychiatry and psychology at McGill University. He has also served as president of the Association des Arts Thérapeutes du Québec.

The importance of an integrative approach in the psychotherapeutic process has been one of Dr Grégoire's areas of study and research. His work has focused on the bio-psycho-social-spiritual perspective, and he has explored the application of this model in group and individual psychotherapy with clients presenting with psychological disorders and life-threatening illnesses like cancer. More recently, to better respond to his patients with post-traumatic and anxiety disorders, he has been exploring the use of EMDR (eye movement desensitization and reprocessing), which also has some applications for the enhancement of creativity. With respect for his patients' artistic potential, he helps to activate their healing by offering them the tools of art media for expression.

Pierre has presented some of his work at conferences and workshops, and his writings on the psychology of art and art therapy have been published in articles and book chapters. He believes that the energy and ideals of creativity can be brought to life through the use of art media, and he is presently exploring the experience of time in the visual arts.

The enjoyment that I find in the creative aspects of visual art and poetry comes from the opportunities that they provide in giving form and substance to what is otherwise but a passing state of mind or awareness.

It often begins with my daring to believe that indeed I have something to say. The risk is also that my work may not succeed in becoming a creative dialogue between material form and what I vaguely experience at first as a project.

The making of art is the exploration of the visual experience and its as yet unknown perspectives. It is an inquiry into symbolic process, an examination of the truth that may remain beyond appearances. In the painting of landscapes I explore the dimension of time, its persistent presence in the mountain motif, and its fleeting presence in the crashing waves of the sea. It is just that fugitive instant I try to seize in an image. In the making of poetry, I find more of a search for meaning and ownership; finding the right word is naming in the service of discovering validation and truth.

As illustration, I will recall that in an art gallery, we can observe how the motions of visitors alternate dutifully between their careful scrutiny and involvement in the visual experience and, regardless of how obvious the work, their irresistible urge to read the title and other written description. What the eyes have just perceived needs confirmation and reassurance to be believed and validated.

These two forms of creativity are complementary. In visual art, the title is an attempt to name the experience. Likewise, in poetry, the power of the words is not only in naming but in making present through the symbols and the metaphors the experience of imagery.

In the making of art and of poetry, these complementary aspects become part of my work. I inquire into the symbolic representation of a reality which is yet to be brought into knowledge and into awareness.

*Passage East* by Pierre Grégoire
Acrylic, 23" x 30"

# FROM EARLY DAWN

With knowing eyes and counted stride
Reaching to one familiar guide
Wild geese know well their traveled run
From early dawn to setting sun

Through errant tides and defiant shores
Through greedy sailors' calls and lures
Homeward salmon climb on and on
From early dawn to setting sun

The morning dew has but one dream
From leaf to brook to tumbling stream
Rushing until its journey's done
From early dawn to setting sun

How will I know my guiding star
Am I astray am I afar
For I stumble as I go on
From early dawn to setting sun.

# $\mathcal{B}$onnie **Hartenstein**

Bonnie Hartenstein has a master's of fine arts degree in painting, drawing, and fiber; a master's in twentieth century art history from the School of The Art Institute of Chicago; and a bachelor's degree in English literature from Northwestern University. She has been teaching painting, drawing, and color theory at the School of The Art Institute of Chicago for 20 years, has exhibited her work nationally, and was represented by Jan Cicero Gallery in Chicago. She is also a published poet.

Bonnie has received grants, awards, and fellowships for her extensive work in the arts. She is an artist and poet who loves abstraction, color, texture, rhythm, metaphor, sound, and images. Both her paintings and poems are about the energy of nature, the Tao, the shamanic journey, and deepening awareness.

Currently Bonnie resides in Sedona, Arizona where she is a Tai Chi instructor and the director of The Center for Balance which offers inter-disciplinary art retreats in nature to expand and nourish the spirit.

Words are a palette for me. They are the colors that create sounds and composition and movement—the essential elements of both my paintings and my poems, creating patterns of sensual energy and states of being.

In both forms I work spontaneously—word to word—color and gesture to color and gesture. Some painters work with sketches, planning and then executing. I respond as I go. But the content of my poetry and painting differs, and although both involve composition, their craftmanship differs as well.

My painting is conceptual. It is about the idea of change and the transitory nature of life. My art engages memory as well as current perception to access my whole experience. In poetry, I respond to feelings or to events, seldom to ideas. I keep a many–paged list of words that inspire me. I let the sensory quality of sounds guide me in representing experience. Although my poetry is not conceptual, an idea may emerge that surprises me into new awareness.

A poem never feels complete. I am always considering changing a word here or there. I can delete a phrase from a poem and use it again to restore the poem to its original form. The finished surface of the poem may suggest the history of the process by its eventual clarity or refinement, but will not reveal the process of creative struggle.

A painting remains a changing form until I determine that it is complete. I keep checking out line, texture, and composition, deciding when all parts are balanced and alive, expressing my concept as far as I can. The painting may look temporary, yet I am sure when I have completed my work with it. Whatever I paint over is always incorporated in the surface of the painting. My painting reveals my internal struggle in its underlying textures, color flows, and compositional shifts.

*Ophelia's Visions: The Lady Eagle and the Reed Pipe*
by Bonnie Hartenstein
Oil on canvas, 5' x 6'

## COWS

Suddenly there were cows
in a crop of trees
sprouted in a cream
and gold
and blackened haze.

And the cows seemed shadows,
apparitions
of an ancient place in
silence,
disappearing
into hillocks.

There were cows suddenly
serene unexpected figures,
horizontal black,
like the trees
were lying down.

## SUNRISE VANQUISHED

And so the glamorous light

Tells the truth
For a brief moment
As it sings
In radiance
Across skies above.

And rose—gold hues throb

Amid dawn's
Fading planes
Of peach
And creamy
Cobalt blue.

Until dark green silhouettes
Of ponderosa pine
And cedar stretch
Into the vastness
Of the opened canopy above

Emerging

Constant
In one's
Fluctuating
Sight.

And it is gone—

Snuffed out by itself.
The grand entrance
Hardly remembered.
The whisper
No longer heard.

photo by Maija Rouvinen

# Sirkku M. Sky Hiltunen

Sirkku M. Sky Hiltunen, a native of Finland, is a graduate of the University of Helsinki in theater studies, and earned doctorates from Catholic University of America in education, and the Union Institute and University in transpersonal psychology and the creative arts therapies. She has published in the USA, Canada, and Japan and lectured in Finland, Russia, Lithuania, England, Switzerland, and Japan. Her articles, *"'I need to be a turtle, reflective, mindful and slow': The Projective Prism of Consciousness in Poetry Therapy"* and *"The Transpersonal Functions of Masks in NohKiDo™"* reflect some of the transpersonal methods, tools, and terms she has created.

Dr. Sky is the executive arts director and the co-founder of the Art and Drama Therapy Institute, Inc. in Washington, D.C., serving adults with mental retardation, developmental and multiple disabilities, and severe behavioral challenges. The founding president of Therapy Theater Company, Inc. and its artistic director for 18 years, she is also CEO of Beyond Mask, Inc. In Virtasalmi, Finland, she directs the Ilmatar Institute.

Registered as an art therapist and drama therapist, Dr. Sky is a mask maker, painter, costume designer, and poet. She is the master teacher of NohKiDo™ and Therapeutic Noh Theater®, transpersonal creative arts therapy methods inspired by the wisdom traditions of the Finnish mythological epic of *Kalevala,* and the spirituality of classic Japanese Noh Theater. She is a passionate landscaper of Japanese–style rock and Zen gardens and has a black-belt in and teaches Tai Chi. A mystic Christian, she lives by faith, intuition, and creativity. She integrates her wide professional repertoire into her work and has dedicated her life to serving persons with mental retardation, who are her spiritual teachers and healers.

**Visual images came first but required verbal affirmation. When I was only about five years old, and before I could read, I began preaching from a colorfully illustrated large children's Bible.**

I joined a group of girls declaiming Finnish folk poetry, *Kanteletar*. Thus poetry, spoken words, became my first love among the arts. Dramatization later on during my drama and theater studies expanded my involvement with words, written and spoken. In my late twenties, I began sewing appliqués. I studied visual arts, ceramics, wood block prints, and watercolor painting later in life. My interest in writing haiku developed along with my love for classic Noh theater which I studied in Japan.

Meditative vail painting and haiku meditation therapy, my latest forms of painting and poetry, focus on the awareness of the present moment as a prerequisite for the work.

Both are respected disciplines with well-defined rules steeped in theory. In my work, I honor the prescribed process of vail painting and established form of haiku. Both are inspired by observation or memory of nature, require quieting of the mind, and allow intuitive knowing.

In vail painting, slowly and deliberately layering and focusing on transparent color, I empty my mind to attain transpersonal consciousness. I rely on the visual memory of the natural phenomenon of light, with awareness of atmosphere and matter, shadow and darkness.

In haiku writing, I hear, see, smell, taste, and touch nature, sharpening my sensory awareness to attain conscious presence. I zoom into minute details and write whatever is sensed, perhaps editing the raw images later for clarity.

Color is the healing element of meditative vail painting; nature's energy is the healing element of haiku meditation therapy.

*Noh Dancer* by Sirkku M. Sky Hiltunen
Meditative vail painting, 24" x 30"

# AUTUMN IN FINLAND

Country horizon;
endless distance of openness –
measured by swallows

With only one cry…
a wedge of cranes passes and
vanishes in horizon

Dusky fall morning –
translucent frost-bitten birch leaves
still hold on

A sudden cry of cranes –
flying away behind the tree tops …
I am still here

The trees are bare –
the rug of shed yellow birch leaves
softens my steps

A few aspen leaves
hold on to make music
with a gust of wind

photo by Robert Oxenberg, Aspen CO

# Judith
# Eisenstadt Horwich

Judith Eisenstadt Horwich is an artist, photographer, and educator whose avocation is real estate design and development. She holds a master of science degree in design from the Illinois Institute of Technology. Her artwork has appeared in solo, invitational, and juried national exhibitions and museums, including The Art Institute of Chicago, and the Spertus, Aspen, Davenport, and Freeport Museums.

A recipient of numerous awards, Judith's work is represented in permanent collections including The Contemporary Museum of Photography, The Warner Brothers Collection, Abbott Labs, and the Earth Art Museum. Her work has appeared in public and university gallery exhibitions across the United States and in Mexico. Catalogues and reviews of Judith's work attest to its quality. Her biography appears in *Who's Who in Photography*.

Judith was a faculty member at Columbia College in Chicago for 15 years. She is now actively retired and working in her studio. She has lectured at many venues including the Chicago Women's Caucus for the Arts and the Art Institute Potpourri Lecture/Tour Series. Judith offers photography workshops nationally and chaired the National Photographic Exhibition, "National Exposure," in 1990.

Judith designs second homes in resort areas in Michigan and Colorado with a focus on the functional and recreational needs of family life. Active in community service, Judith is a reader for the blind and is a founding trustee for the Jewish Women's Foundation of Greater Chicago.

Written imagery and visual imagery, like fraternal twins, are more alike than they appear. Though they communicate in different ways, each conveys meaning and evokes response through metaphor.

My poetic word and artistic line describe a private, internal world. Through these forms, I strive to conjure associative images, feelings, and ideas in my reader or viewer.

The creative act is the same whether I am holding pencil, camera, or brush. The studio is silent. In the stillness, I hear the voices of my twins, emerging from inner depths. These voices, birthed in unconscious process, have lives of their own, taking form in word or picture. In time, I step back, and with conscious intention, hear and see anew. I then rearrange, and go deeper, only to repeat, and repeat again the rhythm of the process.

My artistic expression, no matter which twin I honor, relies on intuition, inspiration, intellect, and emotion. To balance these four qualities is an eternal struggle. When balance is lost, the piece is lost. To express emotion without becoming overly dramatic and intellect without becoming overly analytical is my challenge. To have intuition and inspiration walk hand in hand with serendipity and wisdom satisfies my creative goal.

*Naptime* by Judith Eisenstadt Horwich
Chromogenic print, 16" x 20"

# EARTHLY REWARDS

Naptime for the pawnbroker's daughter
Curled on two hard oak chairs
Pushed together, nearly a protective crib
The crack where they could not meet
Pressed sharply on her spine

Child
Surrounded by lost earthly rewards

Rows of cameras stare down on the scene
Racks of stained overcoats
The smells of former owners woven into the cloth

Unwound watches and abandoned wedding rings
Time and love stilled
Beneath a ceiling of silent hanging guitars

Black metal safes, heavy golden scrolled doors guard
Wooden cream cheese boxes stuffed with envelopes
Filled with an unknown someone's treasure

Poor man's banker
Gently behind a worn brown work table near the sleeping child
Square thick hands tenderly touching the goods
Father places value
Silently, mother in the back room
Record making in the shadows
Counting, accounting for value
Seeing the child through a glass partition

They died without living
Long before their last breath
Surrounded by
Others' lost earthly rewards
Their only reward
The work
Work of counting
While their child lay sleeping

Waiting

# Frances F. Kaplan

Frances F. Kaplan has been an active member of the art therapy community since 1974. She earned a master's degree in art therapy from Pratt Institute in 1976 and a doctorate from New York University in 1985. Over the years, she has served as both art therapy clinician and educator. As a clinician, she worked in several inpatient and outpatient psychiatric facilities and, for a number of years, also maintained a private practice. As an educator, she held the position of coordinator of the art therapy program at Hofstra University from 1989 to 1996. During that time, she spent a sabbatical year as an instructor of art therapy at Edith Cowan University in Perth, Western Australia, a rich experience that provided inspiration for the painting "Over the Rainbow" and the poem "Lost and Found." She currently teaches part-time in the art therapy program at Marylhurst University in Oregon.

Among other professional accomplishments, Frances is the author of the book, *Art, Science, and Art Therapy* and, from 2002 to 2005, was editor-in-chief of *Art Therapy: Journal of the American Art Therapy Association*. A long-time member of the peace community, she received training in the procedures of conflict resolution for violence prevention and taught a course on art and conflict resolution at Portland State University for a number of years.

She resides in West Linn, Oregon, with Martin Kaplan, her husband of some 40 years, and two cats that, in cat-years, have been members of the family almost as long. To her great joy, her son Jason, daughter-in-law Summer, and granddaughter Anika live in nearby Portland and add brilliant color to the canvas of her life.

It starts with an image. Words adhere. The outcome depends upon circumstance—and need.

A painting requires space and materials so that I can "think" with my brush. The words come later—toward the end of the painting—in the form of a title that generally complements rather than describes. Little further attempt is made to translate the picture into words. Contrary to the rhetoric of art therapy that presents visual imagery as the expression of feelings, I experience my paintings as sensation and I am usually satisfied to let them remain in the sensuous language of color, shape, line, and texture.

A poem, on the other hand, often springs from my need to make sense of an intense emotional experience. It is nurtured by rhythm and requires neither space nor special materials, only time and solitude. A metaphorical image embedded in a rhythmic phrase gives birth to kindred phrases. These eventually set up housekeeping on the page, providing a dwelling place for sadness, love, longing, consternation, and contentment. Indeed, rhythm is so integral to the process that I have found a moving vehicle—car, plane, train—offers an excellent incubator for the evolving poem.

Nonverbal vs. verbal imagery, ideas vs. emotions, visual vs. visceral pleasure—these are the poles of the continua that account for the differences in two creative processes. But there are congruences as well. Both painting and poetry satisfy my need for order. They offer a sense of balance and structure that facilitates attempts to extract meaning from the world, and imparts a degree of protection against what is seemingly chaotic and sometimes overwhelming.

Which do I make: painting or poem? For me, they are two sides of the same coin. It all depends upon how the coin lands.

*Over the Rainbow* by Frances F. Kaplan
Acrylic on canvas, 30" x 40"

## LOST AND FOUND

The wind blows the perfectly sculpted dunes
changing them as we watch.
The green waves tug at the shore
making a slurry of the sand with
each advance and retreat.
We use our cameras to petrify the moments
hoping to make them into keepsakes
like the polished stones I once strung
together with knotted strips of leather.

We climb back into the four-wheel drive
and rush up a steep dune, plunging
with a shriek and a gasp down
the near abyss of the other side.
We do this again then
drive for miles along smooth sand
at the edge of water like an undulating
tapestry of green and turquoise and blue.

Somewhere between the dunes and the sea
the knots come undone,
the stones scatter.
Our cameras lie forgotten while

    the wind blows
    the sand drifts
    the green waves
    tug at the shore.

This our benediction.

## MEDITATION

One…one…one
breathing
in
out
molecules
exchanging
intermingling
inside, outside
one…one…
one…
infinitesimal
particles of matter
building blocks of
the universe
compose a
whole
a self
I am made
of borrowed parts
soon to be returned
self, sun, stars,
distant quasars
in this we
are one…
one…
one…

# HOW TO CELEBRATE THE NEW YEAR

Quietly.
Soberly.
Receiving the clear dawn
and the bare clean-sweepness
of January
(after the rococo fussiness of year's end).
Receiving the gradually growing brightness
like the light coming up
on an empty stage
before the play begins.
Waiting.
Wondering.

Ready.

# *Carol* **Hunter Kelley**

Carol Hunter Kelley's life reflects her dedication to the expression of mind, body, and spirit. During her senior year at Smith College, where she earned her bachelor's degree in English literature, Kelley choreographed and soloed in a three-minute modern dance. Her master's is in psychiatric social work from Simmons College. Today she practices Tai Chi for physical, emotional, and spiritual wellness.

In the early years of marriage and motherhood, Carol entered a weekly light verse contest sponsored by Ohio's largest newspaper, the *Plain Dealer.* One of her winning verses was quoted by Bennet Cerf in *The Saturday Review of Literature.* In 1996, her poem "Safety" was selected for *Voices of Cleveland: A Bicentennial Anthology by Contemporary Cleveland Poets.*

Carol received a fine arts certificate in 1980 from the Cleveland Institute of Art Evening School. After many years of volunteering alongside art therapists, she earned a master's degree in art therapy from Ursuline College in 1989, forty years after her social work master's. Carol practiced art therapy for eight years in a nursing home.

Now retired, Carol continues to focus on her visual art, her daughters and grandchildren. She rescued a Lhasa Apso puppy that contributes much frustration, laughter, and love to her home.

Just the other day, my Tai Chi teacher asked, "Do you know how it is when you know it's coming, but you don't know yet what it's going to be, what form it will take, but it's coming?"

He was describing the beginning of the creative process, already in flux as to its form and unpredictable as to its outcome, but happening, nonetheless.

Creativity happens. Once, when I was painting, rather poorly, a watercolor study of daffodils, there appeared between two stems a slender, elegant hand in violet, the color of the background. The hand, by far the best element in the painting, came unbidden and evoked both respect and joy in me, its unconscious creator.

Early in my life and in my adolescence, poetry came to me in what I think of as the "tiddly pom, tiddly pom" manner, as Pooh, of the A.A. Milne classic, described his songs coming to him. As a young adult, I wrote light verse weekly in response to the challenge of prescribed forms or topics in a newspaper column. The specification still left room for unpredictability. When I write poetry, I may reconstruct the form, remove or change a word, eliminate a phrase, create and re-create. In painting, too, I may modify, darkening the area around a flower's blossom to bring the petals forward.

Neither the task nor the inspiration that comes to me predicts the shape of the poem or painting. Images appear to me, not quite formed, like chickens breaking out of eggs with only the cracks showing. Unlike baby chicks, however, my art and poetry newborns are open to variation and modification after they break through their shells.

*Flowered Pot* by Carol Hunter Kelley
Watercolor, 12" x 16"

## THE SUN ON LEAVES

A carefree painter
Splashing flashing
Daubs of silver
On glistening green

## SHOOTING STARS

Crystal tears
Jewels of white
Streaking the black
Cheek of night

## REBIRTH

Beneath the cold snow
Under dead leaves, the crocus
Thrusts its stubborn green.

# $Sue$ **Kuff**

Multi-media artist Sue Kuff has lived in the Washington, D.C. metropolitan area for over 35 years and considers it her home. An escapee of a frigid northern city in New York, she moved to Washington motivated by a desire to have a longer gardening season.

In her early twenties, Sue worked for United Airlines as a flight attendant and later for Amtrak as a trip coordinator. Enchanted by the fashion world, she landed a job as executive assistant to the president of a corporation that owned a major retail clothing establishment, and participated in the development of seven stores. She modeled in in-store fashion shows and gained poise and savvy.

Working closely with designers and artists, she met and married the young artist and illustrator, Mitchell Kuff. For 30 years, they have been partners in their successful graphic design business for which Sue manages and directs design projects including logotypes, annual reports, marketing materials, and signage.

Sue has devoted countless volunteer hours running fundraising events for various charitable organizations. When her niece was diagnosed with juvenile amyotrophic lateral sclerosis (ALS), Sue and her sister founded the Erin Godla Research Fund for Neuromuscular Disease at Children's Hospital Research Center for Genetic Medicine and raised nearly a million dollars for research to better understand ALS and other childhood neuromuscular diseases.

Sue and Mitchell now live and work in Gaithersburg, Maryland, with their two Coton de Tulear dogs. She loves to garden, sew, cook, entertain friends and family, and decorate their home for the seasons and holidays.

The early loss of my mother compelled me to live sensitively in a world of chaotic and unpredictable circumstances. I was a curious child and discovered early the beauty in nature that has been a catalyst for creativity and the art I have made all my life.

Recently I read words from Emily Dickinson that tell my story: "Nature, the gentlest mother, impatient of no child…."

I taught myself to observe the world with patient stillness, enchanted by the different colors of the seasons, the minute details in a leaf, as well as the treasures in a flea market. I learned to collect bits and pieces of inspiration, organizing and editing them until I discover just the right medium for their artistic expression. The pieces might find their way into a collage or a tableau; they could provide the focal point in one of the "rooms" in my gardens, or they might pose for a watercolor or acrylic painting.

My visual art is composed of ordinary stuff that I love to turn into something extraordinary and bold. Food design is just another canvas for me. Dessert, for instance, will start by my spraying a bed of whipped cream right on the platter, then arranging fruit, candy, and cake according to their colors, textures, and flavors on top.

But poetry is new for me. It had always been difficult for me to express my feelings in words. Two years ago, this changed. Completely out of energy and battling a serious depression, I began to work with a poetry therapist. Lingering, unexpressed feelings of anger, frustration and love finally tumbled out in poetic form. Writing with passion and raw honesty every day,

I shaped images, people, and stories into metaphoric verse.

My poetry begins with a few thrilling words that resonate in my mind. With childlike enthusiasm, I watch new thoughts spring forth from barren ground. Imagination bubbles up from deep parts of my psyche. I rapidly organize my words into a list of rough text that I read over and over at least a hundred times. As an external resource for research and verification, Google has become a best friend. I type, cut, and paste, and use the delete key on the computer often to pare the poem down to its essential elements, its ultimate truth, its authentic emotion, its ability to call forth meaningful associations. A common, everyday flower I write about can evoke the image of a special person; a wooden soldier can be recognized as an obedient child. I like to imagine someone else reading my work to test its power to stimulate emotion and help me understand how it might affect the reader.

Painting, crafting, and designing are different. Instead of paring down to essence, I invite the spirit of abundance.

Future projects occupy my imagination. Thinking about them eliminates the blabber-chatter of negativity that can take control of my life. Drawing on my mental library of words and images provides me with energy, stability, and hope.

*Sweet Pea* by Sue Kuff
Watercolor Dyes on Paper, 16" x 16"
Botanical Study in the style of Pierre-Joseph Redouté

# SWISS AIR III
*Dedicated to Tom Hart*

Tickets to the afterlife are issued on this fated early morning autumn day of days.

Flying fast to cool swiss airs and long dulcet days of mountain highs and happiness.

Out of the clear blue sky an unexpected fate let loose a fervid wild raging deathly fire.

Clutching dear darling ones impassioned prayers are mouthed in lonesome silent fear.

Ageless errant rocks witness the silver-winged body crashing through a deep dead ebony.

The famous flashing lighted house is helpless as the unwanted special deliveries arrive.

Tortured turbulent lost lives surrender swiftly to the deep-water depths of black oblivion.

Deep back-bay waters stir with humanness and cry for unsaved lives that might have been.

Gnarled straggly firs watch unsettled waters waving goodbye to every single soul in flight.

Dragger boats collect the tin beached bits of ravaged humanity drifting onto rugged shores.

Split rock epitaphs with one-eleven sights are aimed directly towards a shared immortality.

A tragedy marked with mayflowers and memories in the hearts of true lovers left behind.


# BLISS

On this cranberry bliss morning,
I watch the snow fall from its lofty home,
rocking me in reverie into a quiet heart space.

Welcoming this glorious day with yawning arms,
I see the nimble winter nymphs dance on ice twinkles—
reminding me of a time when joys were simply wonderful.

What is this soft magic that pulls me out of time?
An inspiring vision of possibility? A perfect symphony?
A serenade that lets me fall into the deepest part of my soul?

Out my window, I can see the genius of one snowflake,
all the lacy crystals that bind themselves together to create
a complex and magnificent masterpiece that very few will see.

Looking further, into my winter-whitened gardens, there
is harmony in the blessed transformation that has taken place.
Standing in the pristine beauty of this place, I am stilled and calm.

Heaps of soft billowing mounds cushion me as I fall into my
place of being without being—surrendering to all that is around me.
In snowbound worship, I receive this white communion from the angels.

# BLACK-EYED SUSAN

This femme fatale often sits neglected on weedy rutty roadsides. She can be seen standing on her slender bristly stalk, in the dry wasted sandy places where nothing else will grow.

Blossoming like a dandelion, in a wild space that can't be tamed, this native gal is sure to catch your eye, posing with her beautiful yellow-petal face gazing up at the high-noon sun.

If you look deeply into her dark brown eyes, this little beauty is sure to delight and enlighten you, and show you how wondrous and dazzling nature can be.

As she opens herself, an everlasting future is secured as her rich golden powder is freely shared. All feathered sightseers are welcomed to take away her sweet and cherished treasures.

In her perennially famous sun-flower family, she often lives a lowly plebeian life for just a couple of years. Instinctively, she becomes competitive and pushes out her flourishing rivals.

This hardworking citizen is frequently abused as her sluggish enemies glom onto her sturdiness and herds of swarmy deer devour her for their own amusement.

Unlike many of her neighbors, she is forgiving and offers herself up freely. In our own gardens, we can enjoy her dizzying display and admire her strength to survive in terrible conditions.

When you see Black-Eyed Susan again, please acknowledge her inherent beauty, her worldly contributions, and please give her some decent soil, lots of nourishment and air to breathe.

# *Carole* **Kunkle-Miller**

Carole Kunkle-Miller is a registered art therapist, licensed psychologist, and personal coach residing in Pittsburgh, Pennsylvania. She directed the art therapy program at Carlow College and guest lectured at Vermont College of Norwich University, Naropa Institute, and the University of Pittsburgh, among others. Dr. Kunkle-Miller worked as an art therapist at Western Psychiatric Institute and Clinic and the Western Pennsylvania School for the Deaf. Currently, she maintains a private practice integrating all of her areas of specialty. Her publications include book chapters, journal articles, and book reviews on art therapy and psychology. She has been interviewed by National Public Radio, the Family Therapy Networker, and Working Mother Magazine. Carole provided coaching for the NBA Milwaukee Bucks, and has led many other athletes to achieve peak performance.

Carole's self-expression has been diverse, from performing with an improvisational modern dance company to renovating old houses to creating mixed media paintings. At her website, she publishes a newsletter and a coaching book assisting people to visualize and become their personal best. Being the proud mother of two sets of twins has dramatically shaped her life. Through her family, she has learned the importance of creative improvisation in daily life. She practices yoga and runs to keep her body-mind-spirit alive and well.

When I enter my studio, my mind is completely blank, void of specific thoughts or ideas. I have no expectation of a completed product, but am fully ready to immerse myself in a miraculous process.

Surrounded by diverse art materials, feelings emerge from my heart, like seeds sprouting and then moving with the resolve of germination. The smell of turpentine acts as a catalyst for my creativity; I begin to paint.

Myriad emotions rush through my body and on the canvas; the process is messy and raw. My heart races as I choose brilliant colors and textures; this is an adrenaline filled activity. Totally involved and consumed by the creative process, I have an intimate and passionate affair with the art materials and my creative spirit.

At times, the final product on the canvas is not coherent or does not appeal to me. While paint articulates my darkest moods, the wise, observing self is absent. When the intensity of my mood lessens, I am able to express and articulate those emotions with words. For me, writing is a comfortable reflection, the calm after the storm. Poetry represents the details of my life, and preserves them for me to read, re-read and re-live with clarity. Art and poetry are the right and left sides of my brain integrating a whole concept; they are the yin and yang of my inner self.

Having completed this process of giving creative birth, I have run the gamut from non-verbal to verbal, chaos to form, intuitive to logical. The twin siblings of creativity, art and poetry, have synthesized to create a final masterpiece. When finished, I am finally at peace, feeling fulfilled in a manner that neither art nor poetry can accomplish alone.

*Breath of Life* by Carole Kunkle-Miller
Oils and natural materials, 18" x 24"

# MY STUDIO, A ROOM OF MY OWN

What possessions, meager or extravagant, do I need nearby to amuse me?
What are my essentials?
Examining this describes who I am.
My values, my desires fulfilled or unfulfilled.
A space where no interruptions take place…no phone, no mail, no surprises, no disappointments.
A CD player, a computer, a teapot cooking ideas in a simple manner.
Journals old and new, letters from friends, reprising where I have been.
Art materials, lots: craypas, watercolors, silk paints, glue, sparkly oil sticks.
Creating, dancing with myself, and no other partners.
Where is that woman I once knew, before babies and mortgages?
Obligations retard the wild spirit within,
but the seeds are there waiting patiently with very little prompting.
Books: old favorites, inspirational ones, gifts from best friends.
Seashells and geological wonders, wish charms, remembrances.
Tissues to catch the grief-filled tears.
Candles to warmly lighten the shadows within.
Not many clothes, too much work associated with washing.
Paper plates: this woman is on a mental vacation.
Bare, only the things that make me feel human:
music, poetry, art, inspirational messages from friends,
and mostly, privacy.
I can do what I want, no demands, no questions to answer.
Expressing the inner me, and no worrying about who is there to listen.
I am having an affair with myself,
and I really like this woman,
strong, yet gentle;
I am taken with her.

# *Joan*
# Critz Limbrick

Born and raised in Virginia, Joan Critz Limbrick graduated from the University of Mary Washington with a bachelor of fine arts degree. Joan enjoys as many facets of art as possible. In her twenty-year career as a freelance interior designer, she has created original artwork for many public and private spaces and installations. Her paintings have been shown in solo and group exhibits throughout Virginia where she has won numerous awards. She is a member of Exposure Unlimited and The North Windsor Artists. Her pottery studio and gallery are located in the art center called Liberty Town in Fredericksburg, Virginia. A published poet and children's book author and illustrator, Joan is the creator of Willowbee Press, which specializes in publishing children's books written by artists.

Joan is intensely interested in transpersonal exploration of the self. As an energy healer, Joan has studied with Eric Pearl, Hideo Isumoto, The Eastern Institute of Hypnotherapy, American Institute of Hypnotherapy, and the American Pacific University. She founded the Transformational Center where she practiced transpersonal hypnotherapy and past life exploration. Presently, she is practicing what Eric Pearl calls "Reconnective Healing."

There. The blank clean canvas is before me. Breath held, will I choose to hear all the beguiling thoughts that run through my mind or will I choose peace?

Who wouldn't choose peace, where joy flows free of time and space and material concerns? Easier said than done. I know. I always think I choose peace, but thinking is the problem. Peace has its own vibration. It just waits for me to find it. Peace fills me with nothingness—a free, clear space to do and be anything.

The times when peace slides in and fills my experience bring such joy! Peace lulls me into the process space of painting. Delicious color on my palette distracts me from my need to hang on to thoughts. I may have a model or a still life set up, but I concern myself with the colors, not the form. Form takes shape on its own as I put color beside color...color over color...color around color...color apart from color. Form appears when I least expect it. I am always surprised and gratified with the result. The creative space inside of me is fed with color and spills out words, just as surprising to me as form. It is as if the painting is speaking to me alone in a language my heart fully understands. It is fun and I am grateful. I am a mystic on a shamanic journey.

I remind myself to honor that journey in everything I do. I walk in nature observing beauty and the interaction of bugs, plants, and other animals around me. Without critiquing, I visit galleries and art shows; I read and drink in stories told by history and the imagination of others. Striving to remain fully open to experience, I immerse myself in whatever I am doing: chopping, stirring the pot, making tea, pulling weeds, planting seeds. I listen constantly for that impulse within that guides me down the creative path.

Too many times I have succumbed to the temptation to go back into my work to tweak and hone without taking time to center myself. But really I know that I cannot separate the process of creating art from the process of discovering self. Perhaps ultimately I am the blank canvas!

*You Who Have Ears, Hear* by Joan Limbrick
Gouache, watercolor, and colored pencil, 22" x 30"

# WHISPERS IN THE WIND SING

I cup my hand to my ear
Straining to hear
Hummingbird and sugar bird and dove

The air is sweet
The air is sweet they sing

A burst of light fills my heart

It is in the noticing that I see the wind
A painted picture of delicious smells
Of freshness, cooling breezes
Swaying branches
Swirling leaves and frigate birds
Soaring high above on spiraling currents
Stair steps to the heavens

Gliding fish speak
In the silent depth of the sea
Immerse yourself in liquid magic they say
Notice this azure rippled undulating display
Of changing form and hue and palette
Living forms of repeating pattern
Light and glorious color
Shapes of sacred geometry all around us

My heart swells with delight
At the variety and the wonder of it all

Suddenly I feel worried and burdened with responsibility
But whispers hidden in that same starburst
Sing me a lullaby of clarity

I cannot protect Earth with regretful feelings
Or judgment against myself
Or any other

It is as clear as the azure water
And the sweet breath of breezes
That it is the single eye of me
That sustains and heals Earth
And my Self

Whispers in the wind sing

# Linsay **Locke**

Linsay Locke is a Nebraska-born multimedia artist who received a bachelor of fine arts degree in painting from the University of Hawaii in Honolulu, a master of fine arts in pictorial art from San Jose State University in California, and a master's degree in art therapy from the University of New Mexico. After surviving ovarian cancer she became a licensed art therapist and Reiki Master and currently leads creativity workshops using all the expressive arts. She is the former owner and director of a healing retreat center in Jemez, New Mexico. For the Albuquerque organization, People Living Through Cancer, and for the University of New Mexico Hospice/Home Health Care Nurses, Linsay has been an art therapy workshop leader.

Linsay's creative work history includes interior design, clothing design, and art education. She was an art instructor in California colleges and received the Teacher of the Year Award in 1994 for her work at the New Mexico State Penitentiary. Her chapter, "The Black Madonna in New Mexico Prison Art" was published in *Cross Cultural Art Therapy*. She has had one-person shows, installations, and performances of her work in the United States, Germany, and Canada.

Come close to Linsay's creative retreats and you might hear the drumming, chanting, and music she loves.

My art and poetry share these similarities of creative process: they intensify awareness, bring order to chaos, sharpen intuition, and provide joy in execution.

The differences, for me, are the triggering events, physical requirements, and innate preference.

The visual and the poetic often start from different triggers. My art process results from a delayed reaction to a prior stimulus. There may be no preconceived idea, simply a perceptual response to form, light, color. My writing process proceeds from an immediate gut level response to an emotional experience. It provides catharsis through linguistic symbols.

Space, time, and materials are other variables. Art requires a studio space and extensive supplies. Poetry can be created anywhere; it can spill forth in the bathtub or on the freeway; it is immediate. There is no mess or toxic smell, no stretching canvas or muscle, or strained back. There is no fear of ruining that great, white void of gessoed ground so painstakingly prepared, only a crumpled sheet tossed off.

But—I love the junk and mess. I love translating the visually perceived to the physically contrived and emotionally evocative. I love the action, the smells, physical effort, the treasured objects, and torn images that—with one sweep of the eye—can be taken in and used spontaneously. I can't see a poem all at once. The words are free-floating and ruminating inside my head. I can't touch them, smell them, or shape them with brush and glue. I generally prefer the right-brained language of art to do my talking.

*Abe* by Linsay Locke
Oil, 40" x 48"

# THE WEB II: HADES' CHARIOT

Like a fly caught in the web, I struggle,
reach for the pomegranate dangling there
enticing me
to taste its sweet fruit—
not knowing I would be doomed
to stay and spin my own web—
abducted and torn from life.

Or was it compliance
that drew me in
half-suspecting, half intoxicated
by the pleasure and promised power
of eternal wife?

Nothing's eternal.
This too, shall pass.
Come fair spider; devour me.
Blend my juices with yours.
Let me see through your eyes
the reality of your multifaceted world.
Whisper sweet lullabies as you spin my casket,
your spinnerets flying faster
than my fingers could ever sail
'cross the geography of his flesh,
the hills and valleys of desire
to die in a caress.

Become eternally mine.
Swing higher on luminous gallows
where vistas of hope
swung and unstrung, betrayed and made foolish.
The rumbling roar of hatred
fanned by those promises,
lured instinct down the dry dusty trail
'til trappers ensnared me.

How was I to know that I was the bait?
And he was out there in the wind,
blond hair blowing and billowing across brown eyes—
empty, dark eyes looking up and down,
darting here and there—as if
to tell me of the lies behind them,
while full lips spoke enticingly of love.

# Wendy Maiorana

Wendy Maiorana was an adjunct assistant professor of art therapy at George Washington University from 1975 to 1998. Her presentations at art therapy conferences in Atlanta, Chicago, and San Francisco include, respectively, "Ghosts in the Attic": art therapy with a mentally challenged child who was also grieving the death of her mother, "Tulips and Two Kisses at the Door": art therapy with a man with Parkinson's Disease, and "My Father, the Portrait Painter." Maiorana was also art therapist on the psychiatric ward of Sibley Hospital and at Janney Elementary School, both in Washington, D.C. She maintained a private practice with children and adults. Now retired, she teaches nine yoga classes a week, has taken up gourmet cooking, and continues to do artwork.

Wendy has a bachelor's degree in fine arts from American University and a master's in art therapy from George Washington University. She studied oil painting in Florence, Italy under the renowned Italian painter Walter Fusi and at the Corcoran School of Art in Washington, D.C. At the Boston Museum School of Fine Arts, she practiced printmaking and sculpture. Trained by the late Bernard Levy, Wendy has worked for the past 25 years in watercolor. Her work has been exhibited in juried and non-juried individual and group shows in Washington, D.C. and Maryland. Her watercolors, sold privately, at auction, and commissioned, are in private collections throughout the Washington metropolitan area.

Recently, Wendy has been exploring pastels, struggling to understand those done by Degas. She began writing poetry after reading *Notes of an Alchemist*, a first book of poetry by anthropologist Loren Eiseley. She credits Eiseley as the primary influence on her poetry.

When I considered the variables involved in my writing a poem or painting a picture, I found two essential qualities that relate to both: vastness and rhythm.

Vastness is the source; rhythm, the integrating factor in my artistic work. Vastness is my word for the endless expanse of time and space. When I write a poem, I search for the precise word or phrase that conveys the notion of eternity; when I paint, I grapple with the choice of specific color or form that imparts the concept of infinity.

Even as a little girl of five, I was awe-struck as I sat on a rock in the woods, looking up and out past the tall trees into the unending sky, pondering the imponderables. A few years later at an ocean liner's railing, I stared out and beheld sea and sky going on forever. In college, I studiously explored the writings of the existential theologians. The writings of Tillich and Kierkegaard encompassed the idea of vastness that would eventually underlie all my artistic endeavors. Art helps me to contain and transform my dread of death and my feelings of insignificance in relation to the cosmic totality of things.

The search for rhythm is integral to my process. Syllables, words, and lines lyrically move; colors, composition, darks and lights successively flow together across the paper. Musicologist G. G. Luce tells us that "we are surrounded by rhythms of gravity, electromagnetic fields, light waves, air pressure, and sound," and I feel the need to not only hear "this music behind the words" but to express it through my poems and paintings.

When I write poetry, I work in metric rhythm, drumming out with my fingers the syllabic beat of my poems; when I paint, I work with gestural rhythm, delighting in the physical motion of my hand as it dances colors across the paper.

As I make art, I am reaching for the universe, star by star.

*Mother's Day* by Wendy Maiorana
Watercolor, 22" x 30"

## DAY DRUMMER

Day drummer,
You do us no honor
You beat your palms
Against our soft skin.
We are but creatures, born of fins,
    that leapt the frozen lands.
Given feathers in our headskin
    we hold untold stories of sky,
But your palmbeat wreaths our flight
    with rhythms that wake us
    or put us to sleep
Before we can fly.


## ALCHEMY

I feel our scales
Flat creviced flesh
    of silver-smooth flint
        borrowed from rock,
Our eyes are sun-glint
melting falling feathers.
Birds are moulting
    and leaves are marking
Charred miracles
    to meet our footsteps.

# *Theresa*
# **Kress Marks**

Theresa Kress Marks was born in 1967 in Rochester, New York. She lived in the small, outlying town of Penfield where her parents had the milk delivered weekly in glass bottles. There was plenty of room to wander and explore nature, picking wildflowers and roaming the cornfields. Her parents were avid antique collectors, and brought her and her three siblings all over upstate New York hunting for treasures. She grew up surrounded by creative adults. The women sewed and knitted, designed their homes beautifully, and made all sorts of crafts. The men were inventors. It seemed as though adults were always making things. She became the family artist at home and the class artist at school, though she had little formal art training until she attended college.

She received a bachelor's in fine arts from Saint Mary's College in Notre Dame, Indiana where she spent most of her time in the art building or practicing her balance beam routines. She favored metal sculpture and ceramics and began to study poetry. With a master's in art therapy from George Washington University, she worked with a variety of populations including children, the elderly, adult psychiatric, and adult survivors of childhood trauma. She is the former art therapist for the Center for Abuse Recovery and Empowerment in Washington, D.C.

Theresa lives in Maui, Hawaii with her husband, and spends most of her time raising their three young children. She enjoys yoga, writing, singing, painting, feng shui, and photography. She is currently working on a book about an Indian saint who has touched the lives of children around the world.

There is a peacefulness for me in both making art and writing poetry. I am simply in the moment, striving for that meditative, almost prayerful state to purify my mind and balance my energy. In that state, my mind has space for art and poetry to work their magic.

In both art and creative writing, the process is just as important as the product. I can always throw a poem away and start over or rework a piece of art. With this mindset I give myself permission to begin without pressure. There is no right or wrong in art and poetry. It's all self-expression. And in this way, both avenues are healing. I rarely start with a plan. As I attend to my creative process, I become aware of my inner self—my worries, my dreams, and what most brings me joy.

My poetry is a glimpse into the depth of a moment, like a photograph that evokes a detailed story. When I write a poem I begin with an inspiration, something I want to remember, or want to say. I am sometimes moved to write after reading certain novels or other poets' work, especially when they introduce me to unique styles. I borrow from their style, and begin, often in my head, writing a piece. Sometimes it makes it to paper, sometimes not.

My art process is about transformation. I love to take a flat piece of cloth, design and sew a garment with it. I love to enter a room, imagine how it might be different, and then make it so. I love to capture my children's moments at play or rest in my photographs. As a child, I loved to create special clothing and beautiful environments for my dolls. Now it is for my husband and children and home. A blank canvas is a mystery awaiting my application of color and form. I might recall and try to recreate the play of light reflected on a pond. Anything can be inspiration for my art, and the creative process itself is deeply satisfying. But I will admit that I am happiest when I create something that I think looks good.

I imagine that when my children are older, I will have more free time to write and make art. Both art and poetry are blessed outlets for self-expression.

*Untitled* by Theresa Marks
Acrylic, 16" x 20"

## PRIDE

Toddling
in blue corduroy
unsteady on carpet
protecting
from inevitable bumps
his arms outstretched
her eyes encouraging
he leans and
steps.

## FIRST BOY

My wondrous child
with bright red wavy hair
resembles the great grandfather
he never knew—
who tinkered and built
gadgets of all sorts.
"A man needs a workbench"
was his motto.

This boy is on a mission.
Just today,
he unloaded the dishwasher,
drawers and all,
pulled a painting off the wall,
and joyously dumped
a box of three hundred toothpicks
on the kitchen floor.

Someday he will learn
from his grandfather
how to repair a door hinge,
refinish an antique,
grow a green lawn.
He may build a rock path, a fence,
and maybe, just maybe,
fix something for me.

# Linda McQuinney

Linda McQuinney earned her bachelor's degree in health arts at the College of St. Francis in Illinois and became a registered nurse at Immanuel Hospital in Nebraska. She later received her master's in art therapy at Vermont College. Before she retired as an art therapist, Linda provided individual and group therapy for inpatient clients in acute care, clients with developmental delay, older adults in rehabilitation, and Alzheimer's patients in institutional settings.

Trained and certified as a botanical illustrator, Linda has studied native plants and their habitats in her broad travel and freelance work. She has led nature-related art classes and groups for children and adults of all ages at environmental education and community arts centers in Arizona, Colorado, Idaho, and Montana. She takes great pleasure in sharing her love of nature with her 12 young grandchildren.

Linda's botanical and fine art and handcrafted books have been exhibited in individual and group shows with Longmont Artists' Guild and Denver Botanical Gardens. Her summer studio in the Pacific Northwest, where she tends a small vineyard and orchard and raises native plants, perennials, and medicinal herbs, provides the ideal inspirational setting for her latest passion, gardening. She and her husband share enthusiasm for dancing and are competition-level ballroom dancers.

I am aware of three overlapping variables in my process of making poetry and making art: physical location, mental location, and the art form itself.

The physical, or geographic, location influences my mood and inspiration. I am rarely indoors. My outdoor environment and inner life have an impact on the themes I choose to pursue through artistic forms.

Poetry and art seem to be two sides of a coin. On one side, the words become a specific shape; on the other side, the visual images come out in words. Either way, words and/or images interweave to reveal something drawn from my own life experiences, thoughts, and feelings.

Poetry is the most immediate, direct, and complete form for me; I do, however, revise. Although I have no formal training, I write poetry as an idea reduced to its simplest form, pared down, reflective of my recent lifestyle changes. I enjoy poetry making, even when it is occasionally problematic. Like art making, poetry provides an element of discovery and pleasure that helps me explore territory that might be anxiety provoking.

My current art form, bookmaking, is a much more deliberate process. I have lately included botanical drawing and painting, and illustrated letter forms. I revise pieces over periods of time. I always have several things in various stages of gestation. Reworking is a demanding process that develops my discipline for sustained productivity. Fortunately, I am endlessly attracted to working out an idea.

With three-dimensional media, materials come to life and can become guides for the ideas that follow. The primary source for my images is the stillness of my mind; silence is my greatest teacher. There, I can be with the inspiration or idea and allow the images to come forth.

All my efforts in art are about deepening my relationship with the sacred. My work is about learning to view everything as spirit clad in form. Through art making and poetry making, I have found understanding and harmony. For me, artistic expressions, in any form or process, are the very essence and celebration of the spirit.

*Untitled, #3* by Linda McQuinney
Colored pencil, 11" x 14"

## FIERCE BEAUTY

ageless mounds
of supreme rock
sentinels
of endless change

their jagged edges
tear the sky
or pierce the clouds
with fierce beauty

echoes of the future
unchanged by
any past

# Wendy Miller

Wendy Miller is an artist, writer, educator, and expressive arts therapist. An integrative thinker, she is interested in the language of imagery as kinesthetic narrative. Miller has been an exhibiting artist and sculptor since 1980. She has been an educator in fine arts at San Francisco State University, John F. Kennedy University and in expressive arts therapies at California Institute of Integral Studies, George Washington University, Southwestern College, and Lesley University.

Miller holds a master's in creative arts: experimental and interdisciplinary studies from San Francisco State University, and a doctorate from Union Institute, where she studied the physiology of imagery and health psychology. As a writer, she has had pieces published on creativity and identity, such as her visual/poetic artworks and her clinical findings about medically ill clients, international adoptive families, and multiculturalism.

As a sculptor, Wendy creates installations with clay, glass, paper, stone, sound, ritual, and mythopoetic texts. Influenced by the women's art and performance movements, she exhibited her works in California at Southern Exposure, San Francisco State Art Gallery, Vida Gallery, and Iona Gallery, as well as in numerous outdoor site-specific installations. In 1982, she received an award from Mayor Dianne Feinstein and the San Francisco Commission on the Status of Women for her work titled, "Images From Our Lives."

Since she moved to the Washington, D.C. area in the 1990s, Wendy has exhibited at the Colonnade Gallery at George Washington University, the University of Maryland Art Gallery, and CREATE Arts Center, and co-founded the CREATE Therapy Institute in 1994. She works today as an artist, mentor, and clinician in a renovated carriage house behind her home, part of a healing garden where her clay figures live outdoors among the trees. She resides with her husband Gene Cohen, their eleven-year old daughter Eliana, and their two cats.

I have always written. Writing came naturally for a child journal keeper full of private wonderings. Sculpture came later. I was lured into it romantically as a young traveler hiking through the Andes to Macchu Picchu.

Almost near the clouds, I saw orchids with only thin air to breathe growing out of stones tightly fit together. When I returned to the states, I knew I had to build. It wasn't that I had an image of myself as an artist, but that I felt the need to express myself in form. Although I got into graduate school through my writing, I kept going to the sculpture studio to build bigger and bigger structures.

Writing and sculpting have always gone together for me. My mythopoetic voice speaks in words formed by rhythm and physical relationship, and my sculptures build narratives that tell stories to me. During the 1970s and '80s in San Francisco, I worked as an installation artist using sound, poetry, and sculpture. Even though I described my work in the language of sculpture, my installations always incorporated written pieces, sometimes as ritual, sometimes as studio notes written in clay, sometimes as visual poems carved into the sides of my clayworks.

You Live in the Frigerator and Heartsong chronicle my six-year infertility experience.

Heartsong was written after I lost a long-awaited pregnancy. I have always spoken this poem to the rhythmic fading in and out of Aaron Neville's song of the same title. It soothes me. My words formed recognition, bridged years of silence, grew orchids in skinny places. All of my art is about exploration. I view my poems as word sculptures. I focus on the textural and textual sensuality of experience. I write to bring the physicality of mind-body thinking to the page—sound and rhythm transporting the inner landscape to an outer container. I use my feminine voice to express love, loss, and health.

My artwork is about sculptural space as relationship between the formality of my sensate inner landscape and the formation of physical space. Soul Carriers is part of a larger installation of works made up of cell/egg drawings, boat/carriers, and prayer stones. It both awaits and carries life in slow and arduous ways. My creative process aligns the literal with the imaginal in a context of awe and mystery.

*Soul Carrier #4* by Wendy Miller
Fired/stained porcelain

# HEARTSONG

to Aaron Neville's song

Not enough room to breath
the heart calls
Keep the beast in care
the breathing heart calls:

         *Don't go  please stay*
         *Don't go  please stay*

Pulsing against time
the heart calls
Voice of the womb
the birthing heart calls
out your name

         *This time be different*
         *This time be different*

         *Don't go*
against the pulse of the injury
         *Please stay*
in the inverted canyon
         *Don't go*
breathing heart
         *Please stay*
birthing heart
         *This time*
swollen circles
         *Be different*
twisting circles
         *Please stay*

# YOU LIVE IN THE FRIGERATOR
*For Joshua*

*He was three        I was thirty-seven.*
*I went far far away to Washington DC*

Ring        Hello
Hi, sweetheart, how are you?
You live in the frigerator
        You live in the stove
You live under the table
        You live under the couch
You live in the backyard
        You live in the garden

*It was my sister who said,*
*Come now, Josh, let me talk to Aunt Augie*
*That's a waste of money*        It's long distance and
*you've been talking too long*        Say bye bye

Ring        Hello
Hi, sweetheart, how are you?
You live in the frigerator
        You live in the freezer
You live in the suitcase with my clothes
        You live in the ocean under a rock
You live in the forest on a tree
        You live in the sky on a cloud
You live

*I answered her sternly,*
*Listen, it's my money and my phone call*
*I like talking to him  You may not know what*
*we're talking about but we do*

Ring        Hello
Hi, Josh
Aunt Augie, you live in the frigerator
        You live in the kitchen
You live in the living room
        You live in the pillows on my couch
No, you live in the closet in my shoes
        No, you live in the ocean with the mermaids
No, you live in the trees with the birdies
        No, you live in the sky with the fog
You live…
        You live…

*You live, you love, you cry, you laugh*
*My heart pounds as I hear your voice*
*your love calling me        I change ears*
*rest into the sweaty phone      never miss a sound*
*I have to go soon*
*I don't want to go      I live here, but my heart lives there*
*Month after month in my body*
*a pulse of growing desire curled up against my chest*
*in the warm snuggly            dreaming close to a son*
*Early on, it seemed so simple still, it seemed*
*it should be so simple*


You live in the kitty Mira's tummy
        You live in the kitty Mira's mommy
No, you live in the Cat in the Hat
        No, you live in the hat in the cat
No, you live in Marvin K Mooney
        No, you live in Marvin K Looney
You live far far away all the way to the moon
        You live far far away all the way to the stars
You live far far away and it's time to come home now.

*You live      where the silence fills the giggle*
*warm space empties out of rhyme      Our love knows*
*no time is time enough*

*We move      we travel indoors and outdoors*
*through your room and mine      I look for*
*new hiding places where only you can find me*
*I build on your voice with blue and red legos*
*you take mine      and add on the whites      We*
*enter our own rhythm      You stop me*
*time stops me      the tears      It is your little voice*
*tumbles our love into words:*

You live in my heart
and I think about you all the time
        You live in my heart
        and I think about you all the time

*Every year we say      we will write our story on paper*
*draw pictures behind the frigerator door*
*Age three has moved to age six      and*
*You don't live in the frigerator anymore*

*I wish you could have lived under my table*
*crawling on the pillows I tried on under my dress*
*waiting out the pendulum of*
*my dreams      where months turned into years*
*and dreams turned into tears.*

*Where do the dreams live, little one?*

                *I live in the frigerator*
                *and it's very cold and empty there*

# Joseph Munley

Joseph Munley was born in 1947. He grew up in Scranton, Pennsylvania where he learned a sense of humor from his father, intellectual curiosity from his mother, and imagination from their differences. He enjoyed eating, hiking, singing and the barrelhouse piano playing of his uncle Rags Munley. He daydreamed his way through high school and an undergraduate degree in psychology. After moving to New Hampshire to live in a commune, he earned an elementary teaching certificate and a master's degree in art therapy from Pratt Institute.

The commune experience, lessons from nature, the music of Billie Holiday, work as a potter, puppeteer, and daycare teacher led Joe to awaken to his authentic calling. He shares his love of the creative arts with others to help them lead more enjoyable, creative, and productive lives.

Joe has worked with children and adults using art, music, theatre, and writing for the past 25 years. He has treated people suffering from mental illness, substance abuse, HIV/AIDS, and homelessness. From 1990 to 1995, Joe worked as art therapist at Kings County Hospital Psychiatric Center, and from 1995 to the present he has been the activity coordinator at St. Anthony's Residence in New York City.

As a professional artist, he has done puppetry, performance art, and original community theatre. He has worked with Bread and Puppet Theatre and founded Paper Moon Puppets that performed at Lincoln Center Out of Doors Festival. In New Hampshire, he directed summer workshops that combined building masks and performing original plays outdoors. In 2002, his original mask play "Spooning Song" was performed in New York City, and in 2003 he wrote and directed "Scribbles," a mask play updating Kafka's *Metamorphosis* into the computer age.

I started writing poetry and making art as an adult with similar thoughts in my head: *What will happen if I sit down with this medium and begin? What is happening with me now, in my life, that will emerge as I enter a transitional space and play?*

My first poem was a song lyric that came to me while I was working my first real job, a summer job, to earn money for college, shoveling tons of rubber between giant steamrollers, midnight shift at an asbestos factory. Something in the intensity of this experience, some process in my unconscious, perhaps reflecting an earlier way I had dealt with frightening aloneness, produced a self-soothing lullaby of sadness. My poetry allowed a meeting of the unconscious with words, the tools of the conscious world. The musical rhythm, structure, and lyrics of my songs expressed my feelings.

My art began in a letter to my sister that I illustrated with animals. Words alone could not capture the essence of my living in the woods in New Hampshire. I began to imitate the art of the children I worked with in day care centers to reconnect with my own childhood.

When I entered school to become an art therapist, I used art and poetry to chronicle my journey of discovery. Working empathically with the mentally ill allowed me to integrate some of my own primitive and disconnected parts. Slowly, through writing songs, doing puppet theater, writing children's stories, and later in performance art, I was able to use my creative process to bring into my life all that had been denied access before.

My process in performance art is to wear or become the art or poem. I feel like a child playing with the experiences of being alive in the world in the space where the known and the unknown observe each other and touch. I can trust myself a little more to enter my inner world and the creative space of others and let the energy stored there be expressed. Both art and poetry become my search for self and my place in the world.

*Coyote Moon* by Joseph Munley
Oil pastel on paper, 8 1/2" x 11"

## MILES AWAY

by smoking cigars
and wearing long skirts
she slowly pulled away
from her husband
and curled into herself
riding the night trains of this excitement
past every cleaning
scrubbing
screaming baby
ironing board of a
Tuesday morning
that came her way

## THE NEWS

I'm not sure I can read the paper again
the last time
I bent over the Post
turning to trash on the subway floor
I was greeted
with the click
of empty time
blinding lights
agonizing screams
murderous threats
and the moaning
of the souls
lost forever
to
who cares
drugs
hate
injected
mass produced
T.V. beings
without a sponsor
fleeing from themselves
in terror

## MY CHILDHOOD

When I was three
my father
gave me his gun
my mother the
ten commandments
my sister
let me follow her
to where the houses ended
I learned to fly
and crawl
to escape the incoming
bombardment
I divided my armies in two
and directed their destruction
I chose among the beasts of the house
an average sized lion
and called him Joseph
I befriended the dogs
and survived the long rainy afternoons
I went into the forest
watched frogs in a clear mountain pool
avoided the rattlesnake
and hiked to the morning star
burnt into the distant mountain
I was never seen
When everyone was dead and
winter came
I watched wood flames flicker
packed my armies on my back
and walked away
following
a sparrow's song
darting among the trees

# Concetta **Panzarino**

*The editors, who lost contact with Ms. Panzarino, learned through the Disability Exchange that she passed away in 2001. She was recognized for her "dynamism, insight, inspiration, and wise counsel."*

Concetta Panzarino earned her bachelor's degree from Hofstra University in 1969 and held a master's degree in art therapy from New York University. She was a lesbian with a progressive neuromuscular disease that allowed her movement of only her right thumb and facial muscles. A professional artist and a registered art therapist, she worked for over 18 years with both male and female survivors of physical and sexual abuse. She lectured nationwide on the subjects of disability, homophobia, sexism, and the ethics of genetic engineering.

Connie was director of the Boston Self Help Center for three years and served on their board following her health-related resignation. She also sat on the boards of the Disability Law Center, the Project on Women and Disability, and the Boston Center for Independent Living. President of the board of the Educational Services Center of the Hotel Workers Union, she was also on the editorial board of Access Expressed of Very Special Arts.

To run her household, write, paint, garden, and cook in the Italian gourmet style that she loved, Connie used daily full-time attendant care. Her autobiography, *The Me in the Mirror* published by Seal Press in May 1994, serves to educate persons with and without disabling conditions. She co-authored *Rebecca Finds a New Way* and authored *Follow Your Dreams* and *Tell It Like It Is*, books for children with spinal cord injuries and spinal cord diseases.

After undergoing a tracheostomy, Concetta adjusted to using a ventilator full-time. She delivered speeches in the New England area and live, national radio broadcasts by telephone, and continued to write about her unique life.

We include Ms. Panzarino's essay as she wrote it.

I don't know if one makes art or poetry, or if creating poetry and art makes us who we are, inherently creative beings. I consider myself only a part of the process of creating, perhaps because other people need to be involved in aspects of the completion of my work.

The more verbal part of me expresses itself in writing, and the more ethereal, dreamy, primary-process part of me is expressed in my art. I have always had a difficult time naming my artwork; it is beyond words. Likewise, it is impossible for me to illustrate my poetry, because the images float and shift, often with double meanings. I see snatches of the words in my dreams; I hear them in my head as I go through my daily routine. They almost become a song as I am driving in my van.

Having a disability which has taken away all use of my hands has "handicapped" my ability. I cannot jot down phrases on napkins in restaurants or in notebooks. I have to wait until I have a tape recorder or my computer available. Rarely do I trust writing a poem with the help of a personal care assistant because it may be too personal before it's complete. Since I can't write the poem as it comes to mind, the pieces may stay in my head and heart for days or weeks, and may burst forth whole and perfect when I can dictate.

When I need to paint, I do not have the freedom to just do it. I must have an assistant I trust who will stay out of my process as she moves the canvas or the paper a half inch to the left, a quarter inch to the right, or tilts it forward or backward, as I draw with pen or brush in my mouth. I do not see images; instead, I have a feeling of unrest, an energy that keeps me awake at night if I do not find a place for it to flow. Knowing I need to paint is like knowing I need to eat.

I've heard people speak of writers' or artists' blocks and dry spells. I have never worried about them. Sometimes I have not painted for two years, and other times I have painted 50 paintings in a month. The same goes for my writing. If I really want to create, nothing stands in my way. When I'm drawing, painting, or writing, time stands still. I indulge in creativity that gives me life, strength, and energy.

*Disability to Love* by Concetta Panzarino
Ink on paper, 18" x 22"

## FLUID GLASS

I am fluid glass
stretching toffee-like
   a glowing embryo
taking form.

Do not attempt
   to arrest me
      in this shape or that
by plunging me into ice
   to fix my moment.
I must be tempered slowly
   or I will shatter.

## POTTER FRIEND GLASSBLOWER

*(written for Wayne Houston)*

Potter:  glassblower
pottery:  crystalry
beauty:  vanity
total
concentrated symmetry
    needs must meet
      perfection.
   Arms straight
   muscles taut
      sweat pouring down.
   White hot heat
mind and body meet
   fire rages
   checking stages
   tension time creeps on.
Body pain
   all night long
   tireless energy reign.
Nerves of steel
   trembling real
   opening a door.
     The potter god:
     accepting rejecting
     Judgement Day of clay.

# Barbara
# Sobol Robinson

Barbara Sobol Robinson was the child of a Czech father and a Russian mother, who came separately to this country as children during the tumultuous early years of the twentieth century. Her father's dream of higher education led Barbara to Wellesley College, and her mother's love of poetry influenced her desire to study literature and art. She received her undergraduate degree with honors in literature from Wellesley in 1959. She continued the study and practice of writing and art making throughout her children's early years. Barbara had poetry published in *New Poets of England and America* and artwork exhibited at the Washington Watercolor Society. Her early creative pursuits included political protest art and puppet theater.

Since obtaining her master's degree in art therapy from George Washington University in 1980 and subsequently editing the *American Journal of Art Therapy,* Barbara has turned her focus toward children and trauma. She has pursued this interest during a 30-year career in public mental health. For 20 of these years, she has also maintained a private practice and a commitment to teaching. An adjunct assistant professor at George Washington University Graduate Program in Art Therapy, Barbara has also taught regularly at Vermont College and New York University, and has had several book chapters and journal articles published. Currently, she is working on a monograph on attachment theory, family art therapy, and children in disrupted adoptions.

Barbara lives with her husband in the heart of Washington, D.C. overlooking Rock Creek Park. Her studio and private office are a short walk across the bridge from home. Within this environment, she finds increasing energy for reflection, writing, and drawing.

Images, accumulated over time, are always adrift in my head. They are organized at times according to the psycho-logic of my dreams, but usually they are just there in the service of nothing in particular.

A poem will begin to take form when an insistent idea, and a hunger to tell or speak, combine. Something pushes toward expression. And there they are—all those floating images, new and old, with their power to evoke feeling.

Once in the 1970s I began to write about a summer storm, as a way of commenting about loneliness and the changes my life and my children's lives were going through. A fragment from an old movie came to mind—Lena Horne sitting by a window and singing "Stormy Weather" in Cabin in the Sky (I was about 8)—along with a vivid recall of my mother's passion for movies, and the sometimes rainy nights my mother, my sister, and I would be walking to the local theater. All of it was there, waiting to be reassembled according to the rules, cadences, sounds, structure, and multiple meanings of language. What I mean is: the creation of a poem is mysterious and instinctual and yet somehow focused, assertive, even aggressive. A poem in progress moves through the dark waters of recollection, gathering images according to its need.

Now in making art, something else comes into play: the materials—clay in my hands, for example, or colored chalk on paper. The experience is immediate and sensual, close to the body. Everything must be touched, and I may be driven as much by engagement with the medium as with the mind. Having been trained to rely on my intellect, I sometimes find art making the more difficult and challenging process of the two. But the reward—the object I can touch or want to touch—gives me great pleasure.

*Reclining Woman* by Barbara Sobol Robinson
Clay, 25" x 14"

## REHOBOTH

red moon over
black water

hangs tonight

pulling my heart
toward intergalactic
dark

oh tide me over
tide me over Lord
until the day warms
yellow on my outstretched arms

# *Tana* **Sommer**

A native of San Pedro, California and a longtime Santa Barbaran, Tana
Sommer has worked as an artist for over thirty-five years in California, Ireland,
Holland—ten of these years in France. She attended the University of California
at Berkeley, studying art history and photography. At the California College of Arts
and Crafts in Oakland, she was inspired by two European teachers: Frenchman,
Jacques Fabert and German, J. Krell. She had started painting in a serious way at
age fifteen, encouraged by high school art teacher/artist, Jack Baker. In the 1970s
she studied etching at the Atelier Buri in Amsterdam. In 1995, Tana received a
bachelor's degree in psychology at Antioch University in Santa Barbara.

Tana's artwork has been shown in one-man and group shows in San Francisco
and Santa Barbara, California; Amsterdam and Utrecht, Holland; Paris, Brest,
Forcalquier, and Aix-en-Provence, France.

Tana paints with words, too. Her literary works include illustrations and text
for *The Shy People's Handbook* and *Fruits & Vegetables Etc. – Poems & Paintings
Celebrating Daily Pleasures.* In 1999 and 2000, she edited and published *Voices
Found – a Journal of Accessible Poetry* published quarterly in Santa Barbara, featur-
ing California poets. Her own poems have appeared in journals: *Odyssey, Electric
Rain, Into the Teeth of the Wind,* and *Rattle.*

In 1996, Tana created ArtReach—a one-on-one process of experimentation
to find artistic media appropriate for the individual. ArtReach provides non-
judgmental introduction to personal expression through painting, drawing, clay,
poetry, and dream work and takes place at Tana's studio.

Making art is a lot messier than making poetry! The mental/spiritual process of making each feels much the same to me but the physical paraphernalia involved is quite different.

Writing is lonelier—there is not the company of the vapors of turpentine, the smell of the oils, the rags, the colors and the textures emerging, the tactiles, the gesture of the brush or the wetness of the clay. Taking pen to paper can be gestural, but only within a few inches—it won't be a corporal event, the computer keyboard even less so, although the ra-ta-ta-tah does have a sort of rhythmic presence.

On the other hand, making art overtly involves all the senses, all at once. It's sensual; that's one reason we hedonists do it. We like the feeling, the materials, the colors, the physical realization of what was only an idea or image in the mind before. Making art is exciting stuff because it gets concrete and the end product, like a baby, is something totally new. Making a poem is an under-stated event, more subtle, less demanding on the environment until someone chooses to read it.

Despite the physical differences, I feel the same way when I go to write a poem as when I go to paint. I have something on my mind or deep in my heart and I want to do something with this impelling energy. I may choose to write simply for practical reasons, like that I am on a train, in a car, away from all my supplies, with little time,

or I may just want something very concise as a result—something tidy, unencumbering, simple in form, mailable—like a poem. Poetry writing attracts me by its limits—the limits of a physically restricted medium so that all I can do is focus intellectually, focus as much as possible on the kernel of my idea or nugget of a feeling. In the artist's studio, there is temptation everywhere to go off on tangents, ornaments, physical inventions. When fine focusing is what's important, then, I choose poetry. If I simply must add the visual, then I amuse myself by placing the words on the page in an original manner. A poem, for me, is a way to convey, as in a Sumi painting, the most content with the smallest number of strokes, now words. Poetry, like a self-expanding computer file, only gets to full size when it is opened, read, and thought about. Part of the beauty can be the simplicity and the honesty that comes when there is nowhere to hide.

Before and after I write a poem, I feel exactly like before and after I finish a work of art—only the tools I use are different. The impelling energy has worked its charm; there is a newborn product, something to share with others, and when it's a poem, I don't even have to go wash my hands!

*Skyros, Greece* by Tana Sommer
Oil, 26" x 30"

# MAILBOXES

| | | |
|---|---|---|
| Tell it all | Birth Certificate | One box |
| Ties | Diploma | Contains passion |
| All sorts | Transcripts | Several lives |
| Family | Marriage License | Beginnings |
| Friends | AIDS test results | Middles |
| Bank | House escrow | Ends |
| House | Dog license | Pass here |
| Auto | Passport | Delivered |
| Insurance | Children's photos | by stranger |
| Invitation | Divorce Proclamation | Uninterested |
| Charities | Marriage license | in density |
| Catalogs | Retirement pension | of import |
| 'You Won…' | Funeral 'Home' | Sealed |
| First Class | Escrow | in paper |
| Second Class | Grandchildren | Signed |
| Third Class | Diplomas | Stamped |
| Bulk Mail | Military service | Open |
| Love letter | Marriage | mailbox |
| Foreign stamps | One house | Anticipation |
| Years of life | One mailbox | Dread |
| Go through box | Tells it all | Surprise |
| If box reads and tells | Revolving story | Pivot |
| Bare truth behold | Varies slightly | Once a day |
| Balance, 'bottom line' | Sometimes | Useless |
| Death Certificate | Postage due | on Sundays |

# PEACHES AND GREECE

The best thing about Greece is the peach
and how could it not be so?

Ripening to the sound of cicadas all day,
noble cypress in attendance
olive trees, silver-tipped, shimmering

Sun beating down
absolutely nothing between it and the skin
except the insects' shrill rhythm
Donkeys walk past with tiny bells jingling
to the music of a faraway flute

Bronze sunsets over wheat-toned fruit
Summer heat becomes color
Juice courses under taut skin
Flesh builds into succulence
Enveloped in glorious smell

Those peaches

That Greece

# QUAKE

San Francisco fell down one day
Suddenly the lofts were lowered
And everything joined everything else

Forced to this new level
We met the remnants of more festive days
A bottle, a glass, once whole now broken
All of us broken, inside or out

Face to face with our personal debris
The backyard of our lives surrounds us
After a quake
Old and broken tokens stubbornly remain

# $Ruth$ **Stenstrom**

Ruth Stenstrom is a multi-media artist, board certified art therapist, and teacher who was trained in art therapy at George Washington University and in studio art with a master's degree from New York University. A resident of Washington, D.C., Ruth has directed CASSA—the Clean and Sober Streets Arts Workshop—since 1989. She chairs the Art Department of School Without Walls, an alternative, magnet public high school. One innovation of her tenure there since 1991 has been the annual student production of a "video yearbook."

Previously, Ruth helped to create two artist collectives, P Street Paperworks, a silkscreening center, and its sister organization, the Local 1734 Gallery, from 1974 to 1985. She was also a member of the visual arts faculty of the Duke Ellington School of the Arts. From 1987 to 1997, she collaborated with Norm Davis on a series of performances and art exhibits, including mural-size canvas set pieces for *Rimbaud, Café Noir,* and the *Terra Nova Project,* held in Boston, New York, San Francisco, New Orleans, and Washington, D.C., as well as in Montréal, Munich, and Prague. Her most recent collaboration, "Second Stage Chaos," combined an installation of hanging canvases and a poetic/electronic music score with a dance performance by Anne McDonald and sculptural works by Michael Gessner.

As a good friend of mine pointed out, when you write a poem, you don't have to go shopping for words, and usually there is no messy clean up. Words can happen anywhere.

Not only does painting require advance preparation of materials and space, it also makes physical demands on my body, energy, and emotions. While painting can exhilarate, it can be exhausting. When I work large, my whole body is involved with movement of the paint. I use a lot of water as I paint, spray, and sponge the canvas, imprinting and risking the image with purposeful accidents. In the beginning of a work, the process feels free, but at some point I must make decisions about meaning. I contemplate and then labor over minutiae.

Since I have less ego-investment in my poems, my approach to poetry is more playful and humorous—like figuring out an interesting puzzle or pushing words to extract new meanings. My poems come fast; I get an idea and the words trip along in linear fashion. Poetry is temporal—a time-limited encounter defined by length of page and built-in cadence.

Painting is more open-ended; it is harder to tell when it is finished. The length of time I encounter my images is not limited by the medium. The process of painting is circular and can be hellishly long. My painting begins in the middle, like a tree; it starts with its support, then branches out into potential meaning. The first line seen is often one applied at the end. Unlike poetry, painting shows when it has been over-

worked. One cannot go back to the freshness of that inspired first draft and start over again. While there is joy discovering how new colors relate to old, there is also loss for what has been covered up and will never be seen again.

I start my poems with a phrase or two that have been bouncing around in my head, and write them through, almost trance-like, to the end. Then I switch gears to become the editor and do a little polishing. A poem is easy to conceal; it is a letter to myself, and I can control who sees it. I have freedom to give it away. I can always make copies.

A painting sits on the wall, waiting for recognition or rejection. I must deal with feelings of self-exposure. I am more objective in writing than in painting, so completion is easier. My thoughts can be spliced, computer-corrected, and rearranged. I am happier editing; there is rarely a battle of wills. In painting, I enter mortal combat. I question my abilities, I struggle. If something new occurs that I have never processed before, I anguish between the familiar and the logic of a newer method. I wait for the moment when I am willing to risk.

If painting is my wife, then my poetry is more like a one-night stand. While my poetry is more often about my relationships, my painting is a relationship.

*Second Stage Chaos* by Ruth Stenstrom
Art installation and performance, Montréal, Quebec, 1997
Oil, acrylic, and pastel on canvas, 5 double-sided sections,
6' x 12' total

# DIASPORA

When we meet again as colors
in a dream
or a wood
or the space between that is called
the heavens

how shall the vibrations of our light blend?
Loud and brassy
soft and muted
or not at all.

When we meet again as sounds reverberating in a chord
or the sing song costume of a word
or the wind as it cajoles
the trees

Will we be the melody,
an explosion of noise
or the soft whisper
of dew
falling to the soil?

When we meet again as lovers will you still say hello?

## EQUINOX

In January she looked at the sky and saw crystal
In February she put tea in her honey and waited for a phone call
In March she watched a feather fly in the wind and laughed at spring
In April she wrote a poem in honor of her cat and read it to a friend
In May she changed her mind about everything
In June she was a sister to all people


In July she felt burnt out and thought about escape constantly
In August she slept through a summer haze
In September she opened her eyes refreshed and began to work
In October she wore a mask and fell in love with a friend
In November she fell in love again
In December she looked at herself in the mirror and liked what she saw

# EVE, SERPENT

like

a

s
  n
   a
k
e

  s
   h
    e
    d
    d
    i
   n
   g

i
  t
   s

  s
k
  i
   n

I removed your love

# Christine **Vertein**

Born in Illinois, Christine Vertein completed her bachelor's degree in plastic and graphic arts at the University of Chicago and her master's in art at New York University in 1979. Ten years later, Ms. Vertein became interested in the creative process and art making as a healing tool and completed her post-graduate studies in clinical art therapy.

Ms. Vertein co-founded Open Spaces–Center for Creative Therapies in the early nineties, in Oklahoma City. As an art therapist she conceived Catalysts, a series of hands-on expressive art activities to help her clients enhance wellness. Ms. Vertein recently wrote an expressive activities guide titled, *Campaigning For Me: A Catalyst For Well Being.*

Combining 25 years of experience in management with studio art, art therapy, university teaching, and community education, she designs, implements, and provides experiential art, art therapy, and consultation services to communities at large.

Currently living in Alameda, California, Christine works as a clinical art therapist, writer, and artist. She exhibits in diverse settings and sells her work to collectors and designers. Her work is represented in private and public collections including the Mabee-Grerrer Art Museum. Christine has had numerous solo and group shows. She has been commissioned by different sponsors to create a series of bronze busts, relief sculptures, and constructed paintings.

Variables inherent in the process of creating visual art and poetry are related. The manifestations are diverse. Poetry inspires visual imagery. Form and color stimulate poetic responses.

I hear sound when I create paintings, sculpture, or mixed media. Similarly, the rhythmic sound of poetry guides my imagery. The intrinsic quality of my creative process engages me to connect with the environment. I express my inner experience through the medium; I extend my voice, vision, sound, movement, and soul. In creating poetry and visual images, I select appropriate mediums directed by my senses. The art form is my response to my urge to communicate.

My process is reflected in my poetry and visual art. While bringing new images into being, I simultaneously renew and transform them. Nomadic hunts for resources supply me with materials that have been discarded by construction workers, roofers, garage salers, and plain ol' folks like you and me. My senses respond to various stimuli. A story begins to form. As I continue searching and sorting through the materials, I engage in the subjective process of selection and rejection. Words come to mind. I silently recite and connect them, then store them in my memory.

I feel fulfilled as I adopt the discards and bring them home to my studio. I place materials and words into various formats. I give them focus and a space of their own. Their significance is transformed from discarded to accepted and functional. I shift their place until the composition feels balanced. Each additional element, be it word or tangible object, contributes to the whole. When I am satisfied with the gestalt, I stop. Then I might brew a strong espresso, eat a crunchy apple, or begin another composition.

Key elements motivating my work are the urge to express new experiences, sacrifice old ones, permit play, and enter new realms. Presenting a changed reality reflects my connection to truth in the present.

*Concrete Sky* by Christine Vertein
Baltic birch, plaster, acrylic, 2 1/2' x 2 1/2' x 3'

## STILL LIVES AND LANDSCAPES

Mellow like cocaine, melting
existing sensitivities at the Max
Songs are out to get you

Alarm dog buzzing by the sites
fussing with its robe
tigers and dawgs mostly made of paws

Pause beCause alls real

fishin    reelin
points of roddings
hookers blinkin at the lites
Sanctuaries  :   reds and whites
downing bobbers
hooked (a fish?)  on salts
Spilling capsules    Net it!

fragmented portraits
Oval rounds

Ejaculated soft and flimsy
Colors matter non and blurry
Speed is slow again    Taffy pulling time
Souls of such a puzzle piece
Ironic is the matter.

Special women certain types
Smokers  -  drinkers smart sleek cats
clothed short skirted meaty
sleek or chubby
money hungry babes
Grass, happy high ludes cocaine
all accessible again
Good Music
– black              warm
Smelling of oil scents  –   strawberry

                                        Vanilla

                                          Honey dew.

# David G. Vickers

David G. Vickers is a Michigan-born artist initially trained in sculpture at Central Michigan University. He taught art in South Carolina and Pennsylvania and was twice invited as a guest artist to the Pennsylvania Governor's School for the Fine Arts. After completing a master's degree in art therapy at George Washington University in 1984, David spent 13 years working in clinical settings and with the public schools of Dade County, Florida.

Like many other artists, David has been enterprising in a variety of day jobs. Having worked as a framer, gallery manager, art importer, and art therapist, he was also, for five years, the sole proprietor of "Two Hands 2," providing skilled painting, carpentry, cabinet-making, and renovation services to residential customers. Since 1999, David has taught art full-time at the progressive, independent Lowell School in Washington, D.C.

As an artist, David participated in numerous juried and individual exhibitions in Washington, D.C. and throughout the mid-Atlantic region in the 1980s and '90s. He established a following for his color field paintings and his miniature boxes, many of which now reside in private collections as well as in the permanent collection of the Pittsburgh Center for Arts and Crafts.

In 1995, David began to focus on landscape painting, devoting his work to miniatures on paper and canvas. He has painted in the northeastern and southwestern United States and in France.

David continues to paint and exhibit in the Washington, D.C. area.

I paint mostly because doing it feels good and write because I like the results. I enjoy the act of painting, and I expect my paintings to reveal that act: the steps, the layers, the marks and erasures, the development of the paint as a point of departure for the viewer.

The benefit of the painting as an object is as much in its reference to that process as in the image itself.

Not so in writing. The process of writing is a labor I try to conceal. Only when I employ what I view as the most visual or felt elements of writing, such as alliteration and meter, do I feel the freedom of the process, the spontaneity, shared with the kind of *alla prima* painting that I do.

Representation is the great battleground of postmodern work whether literary or visual, and I feel that both poetry and painting are well suited to representation that exceeds the object through metaphor. It is poetry that has helped me to keep open a window for metaphor in the painting process, and it is painting that has kept a respect for formalism in my writing. Meaning is important. In both media, I want meaning to be allusive, not direct. The work should suggest an affective moment as an image. I believe writing and painting have a great deal in common as conveyors of metaphor.

Despite inherent difficulties, I think there is validity in art that combines image and text, and I look forward to producing such work. Language is image and image is language, much as liquids and solids are states of the same matter. I don't concern myself with the tedious debate in the art criticism of recent decades, except perhaps in the ways that language can limit image, much as when you freeze water.

I use words in poetry less to present ideas than to corral an image, and I am willing to stretch the limits of language to go after that image. I create an atmosphere, a context for the reader to develop his own image, his own text. Thanks in large part to deconstructive criticism, the same can be said of painting. The image is an equal player in the process of developing text. I like to think that any successful artistic endeavor is one that unfolds an invitation to the viewer to become a participant, to create the text. That is what I do as a poet and as a painter.

*Untitled* by David Vickers
Acrylic, 4" x 6"

# CAROLINA/CALIFORNIA/LOVE

From between the Carolina pines
come your words in showers
and sliding winds
over ochre and dry dying grass.

Starry shells and silver tiny bells
come tinkling off your coast,
sea words and spiney-finned-blue–fish-words
fly over dry Carolina.

In you there is
morning wind, evening tide, swelling high river,
sliding wind, take-me-riding wind,
on top of trees
and under stones, and the riding ways
of the kite.
I
flying on the tail of your words
in the morning, come rolling,
I dancing
come flying above pine…

I am happy,
come tinkling off your coast,
oh starry-shell silver-bell
California words of love.

# HOME

It's a small place we occupy,
but like the hawk
who sees much farther than the space
from which he flies,
we look beyond ourselves and see ourselves
out there.
A nest,
some twigs and twine
or place in time where we grew up
and wasted time in walks and runs away from home.
It's where the heart is,
home is bed beneath the light,
is path gone out of sight, is tunnel
where we lie in wait
for the rest of life.
Can't get up, get out
get on that cliff with bits of nest
still tangled on my leg,
but ready to fly…
it's enough just to say I left that place
and carried away in my flight
the very things that kept me there.

## KEEPING TIME

The moment's not elusive,
no illusion of importance in its passing.
Instead a chance to ponder comes, a chance
to pause and linger on the clock-face
as it turns.
A chance to stretch the hands that count the minutes
and the hours
till they melt and pass through my fingers
to the floor,
And how, now, to face this silent telling
of matter as it passes through my fingers.
How to know that real is real
And past is passed
Or now is now, not gone or coming.
How to know the motor turning all these things
and me,
how to trust, how to trust
when importance and impatience melt and
puddle below the clocks,
and clocks cease to tick or take a second
at a time and topple from the towers
to the bottom and turn to trickling now,
and tremor, tolling slow and simple
tempos to the end.

# Katherine J. Williams

Katherine J. Williams earned a bachelor's degree in English from the University of Wisconsin, and a master's in art therapy, a master's in psychology, and a doctorate in psychology from George Washington University. She directed the Art Therapy Program at George Washington for over 20 years and is now an associate professor emerita. She has also taught at Goddard College, Vermont College, and Naropa University.

Recipient of the Distinguished Service Award from the American Art Therapy Association, Dr. Williams has been active in the field of art therapy education. She has written articles on art therapy and has lectured in this country as well as in Italy and Japan. A graduate of the Washington School of Psychiatry's Group Psychotherapy Training Institute, Dr. Williams is currently in the private practice of art therapy and clinical psychology in Washington, D.C. and Falls Church, Virginia.

Katherine has been a longtime member of a clinical consultation and reading group and fuels her interest in poetry, literature, and film by attending writing workshops and being an ongoing member of a film discussion forum and a writing group. She is knowledgeable about elegant, healthful cooking and enjoys hiking and distance swimming during her Vermont summers.

Because I do not have a natural talent for rendering likeness, I have to push into the process for hours before I finally make an image that satisfies me.

I can't imagine something and simply create it—I have to have pen or pencil or paintbrush in my hand, make a mark, react to that mark, make another, then another. This kinesthetic visualization is time consuming and frustrating, and almost always leaves me disappointed, yet fueled for another try, loving the swish of the brush, the scratch of the pen, the sweep of color spilling across the page.

When I am working on a poem, the experience is somewhat different. I often have an idea when I start, and when I get inside that idea, there is a little poem pocket in the back of my brain where the poem keeps writing itself. While this pocket is filling, I am more alert to the corona of meaning surrounding everyday life. It goes something like this: On a summer day, I repaint an old chest in my backyard, noticing the bugs impaled in the paint, as if in amber. I let my mind run to those older insects now in necklaces, dangling between the breasts of women through the centuries, and I watch the hairs from my brush pass over the spots where I tried to sand out old brush hairs from the layers of color below. I notice a human hair, and think of the rest of the hair on the head of the man or woman who painted the last layer, the hair that has now turned white, or burned in the crematorium, or decomposed in the ground. And I do not brush away one of my own hairs as the wind blows it into the fresh white paint. Later, my hands smelling of turpentine, I empty the pocket, and the poem pours out onto the page.

I am more confident with words than with images, but once I traverse the terrain of resistance, the visceral feeling of creating is quite similar. That quiet place out of which come both words and images is buried far beneath the alternating layers of inertia and busyness that are my defense against confronting myself at the center. Getting to the "flow" place Csikszentmihalyi writes about is like jumping over a chasm into the unknown—yet on those rare days when the leap is taken, in the sharp jolt of landing, I realize I have arrived home.

*Memory Collage* by Katherine Williams
Collage, 11" x 17"

# TALK TO ME ABOUT REVISION

Words tossed in casually
to get from here to there
become the frame
on which the poem is built

the way the ragged end of brie
dropped into the basket
becomes the heart
of the picnic when sliced
with two ripe pears.

Moving a phrase
is a balancing act
like slipping kindling
under the logs
while the fire is burning.

Three solid lines I savor
no longer fit
but will not leave

the way the sweet sharp twist
I feel when I think of you
will not be revised
for another love.

# DELIVERANCE

I
To the child in bed
the moving rectangle of light
slides across the ceiling,
the chair, a corner of the bed,
settling askew
as the motor idles
outside the window.


Waiting in the dark
for light to soften
her secret terrors,
the child warms
to the familiar chilly
clink of glass
as the milk is set down.


II
This morning, in the dark,
the woman senses the light.
She hears the car
gliding down the street,
bringing some version
of the world
to each house.

She allows herself,
for a moment,
to slip into the old promise
of an orderly universe,
all evidence to the contrary.

# SWIMMING HOME

I slip into the morning water
breathless
as in my first waters.
With a gasp
I'm born again
flailing
until I settle into a rhythm,
my arms breathing the water,
the cold dissolving my body.

I stitch my way
in a disappearing seam
across the lake.
From long ago
I hear the women singing,
*leaning, leaning,*
*leaning on the everlasting arms.*
On shore, I drown in disbelief,
but here, in this moment,
my body believes.

Lifting my head
I glide
as I watch
the flat forgiving surface
stretch to meet the shore.

I turn, heading back,
stitching a path into the day.
Floating in the shallow water
prolongs my refuge.

When I stand,
it is as if for the first time.
My arms battle the air.
I reach for my towel.

I do not remember
the way home.